SURVIVORS
OF
SUICIDE

SURVIVORS OF SUICIDE

RITA ROBINSON

IBS Press
Santa Monica, California

IBS PRESS
744 Pier Avenue
Santa Monica, CA 90405
(213) 450-6485

IBS PRESS FIRST PRINTING, 1989

ISBN: 0-9616605-5-4
Library of Congress Card Catalog Number: Pending

Manufactured in the United States of America

for my parents

Mary Elizabeth and
Starling Clark Robinson

ACKNOWLEDGMENTS

My thanks to BettyClare Moffatt and Laura Norvig who share the vision of a caring society offering love and understanding in the face of adversity.

My gratitude to the many survivors who shared their stories with me and the professionals who took time to discuss and impart their knowledge so that others may have a more enlightened understanding of suicide and its aftermath. These sharing individuals include: Bem P. Allen, Terrence W. Barrett, Janet B., Alan L. Berman, Ben Zion Bergman, Judith Bernstein, Dana Brookins, Robert Carney, Robert Cancro, Mary S. Cerney, Peter Covas, Leslie Elliott, Gary Emery, Norman Farberow, Martin Finn, Chip Frye, Robert Gable, Marvin Goodman, Elaine Gracia, Phyllis and Covell Hart, Norman Hearst, Sam Heilig, Paul Hilsdale, David Hoffman, Taffy Hoffman, Mamoru Iga, Ira and Jeanne Jacoves, Jan Kelso, Gerald Klerman, Monette L., H. Newton Malony, Jean Mathews, Richard T. Monahan, Diane C., Mary Ortega, Michael L. Peck, David P. Phillips, Jane Frances Power, John Przybys, Havanpola Ratanasara, Richard J. Seiden, Jack Simonson, Dennis Smith, Jan van der Wal, Carol V., T. Wilson, Carl Wold, Adina Wrobleski, and many others who sparked conversations that made me dig for answers.

CONTENTS

PREFACE

My own interest in suicide prevention, and help for the survivors, began with a series of articles on suicide that I did as a reporter for a metropolitan newspaper on the outskirts of Los Angeles.

At that time suicide was just on its way out of the closet, and one of the first groups for survivors of suicide had been formed at the Los Angeles Suicide Prevention Center.

At about the same time the articles ran, the twenty-six-year-old son of a close friend committed suicide. It was devastating for everyone. His death fit no pattern (as many don't). He had just returned from a successful tour of Russia and Japan with the musical group, "Hiroshima;" he wasn't into drugs; he had a stable family life; and he was young, handsome and intelligent.

Nevertheless, he hung himself, leaving family, friends and acquaintances to travel in foreign territory without the benefit of knowing the language. While no one is ever prepared for suicide, it is my hope that this book will help both survivors and the general public acknowledge and cope with it.

Rita Robinson

FOREWORD

Two days after I was given the manuscript of *Survivors of Suicide* to read, I met a man whose son had killed himself just the week before. He said, "I'm reading a book a friend gave me, and it is helping a little." I was happy to be able to say to him, "I have another book for you. It's not out in print yet; you can read my copy." It made me feel a little better to know I was putting something in his hands to help him in the days of grief that were before him.

"Life is difficult." So begins *The Road Less Travelled* by Scott Peck. I knew when I read that first sentence that it was a book I wanted to read. I had the same feeling when I began reading *Survivors of Suicide*. This is a book that needs to be read. It is likely that if you are reading this book, someone you know - and love- tried to, or did, commit suicide. I have been a therapist for nearly thirty years, and I have found that often the best therapy may be to hear and be comforted by someone who has suffered the same trauma.

In this book you will hear from those who have suffered as you have. You will read their stories, and in between the lines feel their pain, their outrage, their despair and their hope.

Suicide is a compelling and personal tragedy. It leaves survivors bewildered and confused - and usually guilt-stricken. "Why did they do it?" "If only I had..." are phrases said over and over again.

Mary had visited in our home just a few days before she got into her car in her garage and turned on the motor. She was a young mother of three children, and when her wonderful husband died suddenly of an unusual illness, she had become depressed. Her doctor had planned to hospitalize her soon. If only we had had her stay with us, if only....

Survivors of Suicide is a good and necessary book. You will need it if:

You have lost someone through suicide

Someone you know has tried to kill themselves

You have contemplated suicide yourself

A friend, relative or acquaintance is a survivor of suicide

You are a counselor, clergyperson or mental health professional

Comfort comes to us in many and diverse ways. This book has been a comfort to me; I pray it will be so for you.

Phyllis Hart, PhD.
Pastor, First Presbyterian Church
Author, *Concurrent Counseling*

SUICIDE WARNING SIGNS

1. Suicide threats.
2. Previous suicide attempts.
3. Statements revealing a desire to die.
4. A preoccupation with and asking questions about death.
5. Getting affairs in order.
6. Giving personal effects away.
7. Personality changes or odd behavior.
8. Withdrawal, apathy, moodiness, anger, crying, sleeplessness, lack of appetite.
9. Loss of interest in usual activities.
10. Tendency toward isolation.
11. Statements about hopelessness, helplessness or worthlessness.
12. Mental depression
13. Sudden appearance of happiness and calmness after a period of some of the characteristics listed above.

SIGNS OF DEPRESSION

1. Persistent sad, anxious, or "empty" mood.
2. Feelings of hopelessness, pessimism.
3. Feelings of guilt, worthlessness, helplessness.
4. Loss of interest or pleasure in ordinary activities, including sex.
5. Sleep disturbances (insomnia, early-morning waking, or oversleeping).
6. Eating disturbances (either loss or gain of appetite and weight).
7. Decreased energy, fatigue, being "slowed down."
8. Thoughts of death or suicide, suicide attempts.
9. Restlessness, irritability.
10. Difficulty concentrating, remembering, making decisions.
11. Physical symptoms, such as headaches, digestive disorder, and chronic pain that do not respond to treatment.

INTRODUCTION

Every year in the United States, at least thirty thousand people kill themselves, and for everyone who commits suicide, their deed reaches out to touch dozens of acquaintances, friends and family members.

Until recently there was little help for these survivors of suicide — those left behind when someone takes his or her own life. But like other closeted subjects, people are beginning to understand suicide in a new light, although one that casts many shadows.

As this door opens and light starts pouring into the closet, shadows begin changing form, but they aren't completely eliminated because much is still not understood about suicide. Controversies exist because suicidologists and mental health professionals, as well as clergy from various faiths, are not in complete agreement on the causes, consequences and prevention of suicide.

French sociologist Emile Durkheim's definition of suicide, which he penned at the turn of the century, is still in wide use today among mental health professionals: "The termination of an individual's life resulting directly or indirectly from a positive or negative act of the victim himself which he knows will produce this fatal result."

Many in the mental health profession believe the majority of potential suicide victims are suffering from undiagnosed schizophrenia, manic-depression or severe depression, and that medication to get the brain chemicals functioning properly again is needed before therapy can have any effect. Others place the figure for depression-related suicide lower.

This disagreement is caused, in part, by an age-old division in the mental health community between medical people, who tend to treat depression as endogenous, or coming from inside the body, and psychotherapists, who tend to treat it as being caused by outside or environmental forces — something which can be resolved by talking through the problems. Most modern therapies acknowledge and combine both of these viewpoints.

What is certain, though, is that never has there been such widespread interest in the study of suicide, and out of the flurry of research and new understanding will come better and more supportive help for those touched by suicide.

This book is for the survivors, for they too are hidden deeply within the shadows. Through their stories recounted on these pages, they will make it abundantly clear that they need a community capable of offering support, help, love and understanding instead of the age-old taboos, stigmas, half-truths and ignorance that have, in the past, kept the closet door so tightly shut.

Discussions on suicide prevention, the latest suicide research, history, and views from the clergy are included in this book, but it is the survivor who speaks most eloquently. Each story is unique, and yet, there is a common thread. The survivors are all thrust into areas of grief that send them to the edge of despair. But by peering over this edge, they sometimes see things that are obscure to others. They become our teachers.

Because of their insights, they are demanding that our institutions, politicians, philosophers, health professionals and religious leaders begin the process of coming to grips with suicide.

"We just have to stand up and scream at them," says one professor of psychology.

Taking one's own life is not a single issue matter. It tugs at the fabric of other social conditions that have long been neglected, and demands our attention and compassion.

When I wrote one survivor whose twenty-one-year-old son had committed suicide, asking permission for an interview, she answered, "I would be happy to speak to you — in hopes it will help other people. It helps my healing to help others to understand."

Her words were echoed by a twenty-nine-year-old man whose brother had committed suicide. "Talking about it might help someone else who's going through a similar situation," he said.

The coping mechanisms and stories of the survivors of suicide make up the bulk of this book. I only hope they are related here with as much honesty and generosity as they were told to me. It's my belief that only through openness, education and love can we help the survivors, and we are all survivors.

There is no appropriate moment in time that lessens the impact of hearing that a loved one or an acquaintance has committed suicide. The event is shattering at any hour of the day or night.

It violates the strongest of emotions and urges. It violates our purpose — the will to survive. Nonetheless, at some point in many people's lives this menacing stranger will grip their hearts and rip apart their emotions.

Unlike other forms of death, which are followed by established patterns of grief, suicide leaves the survivor wallowing in unchartered areas, as if plunked down in the middle of a dark ocean in a rowboat without a paddle.

Despite headline-making suicides, and the fact that thousands of people commit suicide each year, when it hits close to home people feel as if they're the only one who has ever been touched so powerfully by suicide — a singular entity engulfed with overwhelming feelings of grief, shame, anger, guilt and frustration.

Until they are touched by it, most people do not give suicide a second thought. They seem to prefer to believe that it is a rare occurrence. I'm constantly reminded of a conversation I had with a young professor of journalism. We were discussing writing and I mentioned that I was working on this book.

"Seems like your market would be quite limited," she said. "I've never known anyone who committed suicide."

Not wanting to shatter her youthful naivety completely, I only mentioned that in the United States approximately thirteen people in every one hundred thousand commit suicide each year.

These figures don't take into account the unreported suicides or those who lead suicidal type lives with death attributed to accidents and/or alcohol and drug abuse.

Suicide is a stranger to no race, creed, religion, age group, income or education level, and people have been taking their own lives since the beginning of recorded history.

The "why" of suicide is the big question — both for researchers and those left behind. I've seldom met a survivor who could pinpoint the reason for a person's taking his or her own life. This unanswered question is one that leaves people in turmoil. Even when a suicide note is left it rarely touches on the true cause. The victim's thinking process is too distorted by then. Additionally, survivors constantly question the "why" of their own reactions to the suicide.

Janet B., a former volunteer at a suicide prevention center, recalls that four years after her brother's suicide she was driving down the freeway and began crying and screaming about the incident.

She had kept her feelings of rage, anger, grief and guilt bottled up for so many years that even though she had worked at the center for two years, she still wasn't over her own personal trauma. Janet is not an exception. Although new research indicates that survivors of suicide recover at about the same pace as those who lose a loved one to any unanticipated death, the mythology of suicide tells them that they should suffer longer and differently.

It is natural for people who have lost a loved one in an accident or a serious illness to grieve periodically throughout their lives, but it softens through the years, and so it does for the survivors of suicide.

It is the onset of the death, the first hours, days and months, that create such a muddied mosaic for the survivors of suicide.

When Janet received news of her brother's suicide she requested that her fellow workers not send flowers or cards or offer to help, as they had done the previous year when her mother had died. "And I don't know why I did that. I don't know whether it was because if they didn't do anything I wouldn't have to deal with it, or if there was a part of me that was thinking, 'He doesn't deserve the same as my mother.' I don't know to this day."

Not only is the grieving family member or friend left with a plethora of unanswered questions, but they must face the ignorance of friends and acquaintances who believe much of the mythology of suicide.

I was discussing suicide with some acquaintances at a nearby restaurant recently when one of them, a woman, said she had a friend who had been married twice and both husbands had committed suicide.

The gentleman sitting with us snidely remarked, "Wonder what she's doing to drive them to suicide?"

It was like talking to a blank wall trying to explain to him that no one directly causes another person to take his or her own life.

Another woman who claims to be a born-again Christian, and whose stepfather committed suicide several years ago, once remarked, "Well, we know what happened to him. He went straight to Hell."

Most religious bodies today, while not endorsing suicide, take a more enlightened view. The idea of punishing someone who has already been living an internal hell-on-earth seems rather cruel, especially for the survivors.

There was a time when people who attempted suicide were treated far worse than criminals, and families of suicide victims were disowned by a community. That legacy may be past, but the stigma and taboo still weave through society like a yellow river of poison.

What is significant is that never before in our history has there been such an interest in the causes and prevention of suicide. Society is demanding answers, clearer understanding and more gentle treatment of the suicide victim and the survivors.

Throughout these pages, I will try to dispel many of the myths commonly associated with suicide, and to offer instead, some of the truths that are changing the shapes of the shadows that have stayed hidden for so long in the closet.

Survivors
Of
Suicide

1

THE IMPACT: SHOCK, GRIEF & GUILT

SUICIDE hits below the belt. We are often somewhat prepared for the deaths of elderly parents, or friends and relatives with serious diseases, although that too is painful, but we are seldom aware that suicide will touch us.

Many support groups have been established for widows and widowers, for those whose loved ones have been murdered and for parents whose children meet untimely deaths, but support groups for survivors of suicide are more rare than abundant.

Thanks to the efforts of people like Dr. Elisabeth Kübler-Ross, the pioneer in the hospice movement who helped enlighten the public on death and dying, death is now seen as a more natural part of life, but suicide isn't. Although the stages of grief have been explored and have become universal, they come in different forms when death is caused by suicide.

In any type of bereavement, people may experience stages of emotion ranging from alarm, disbelief and denial, to anger and guilt. Finding a source of comfort and eventually adjusting to the loss become important goals.

When suicide is the cause of death, however, these stages are taken apart, turned upside down, backwards and shaken as if by an earthquake.

When a person loses a spouse to an accident or illness, well-meaning friends and family often spend time with the bereaved just listening to them. People shy away from suicide survivors, however. Frequently they don't know how to begin a conversation. One very close friend of a woman whose young son had committed suicide, told me she didn't go visit the woman because, "I just didn't know what to say."

When I attended the funeral of my friend Beverly, who committed suicide several years ago, I too was stuck for something to say to the survivors. The words spoken at the service had no meaning. The grieving family seemed like puppets to me. It was as if I was taking part in a daydream — half awake and half asleep. Nothing seemed real.

To this day, I don't think of Beverly as dead. She had been my next-door neighbor when our children were young. I remember her as being wonderful with her own five children, and she always had a houseful of other people's kids.

Her first husband left with another woman three days before Christmas one year, and she eventually remarried when her children were in their teens. The marriage seemed happy and stable and when I visited her in her new home, her life seemed better than the earlier years. But a few years later, after her children were grown and married, I received a call from her husband telling me that Beverly, who worked for a diet doctor, had been missing for the weekend and that they had found her body in the office where she worked.

She had gone there on Friday, taken a quantity of pills and was found dead Monday morning when the staff came to work.

Several years have passed since her death, and to this day it does no good for me to try to understand why she did it. She had a great sense of humor and it was fun just being with her. The death left me with a feeling of emptiness, and I wish now that I could talk to the family, take a more enlightened part in her funeral, and lay her memories to rest.

I know I can never know why she committed suicide or what was going on in her mind during those last few hours, minutes and seconds.

But survivors of suicide always ask themselves that question, and they are frequently asked by well-meaning friends, "Why do you suppose he [or she] did this terrible thing?"

One woman, whose daughter had committed suicide, wrote Ann Landers saying, "When something like this happens, there is tremendous guilt among family members and everyone close. The most painful question for me was, 'Why did she do it?' Every time I am asked it makes me feel that she would still be with us somehow, if only I had paid more attention or if I had stayed home that day, and a million other if's. Just thinking about it now makes the pain come back, and it's as bad as the day it happened.

"What I want to shout to everyone is that 'I DON'T KNOW!' Don't they think if I had seen it coming I would have moved heaven and earth to prevent it? The girl was my heart and soul."

Perhaps those who ask the question, "Why did they do it?" are trying to find answers themselves, feeling that those close to them might also be vulnerable. The death of a young person, for instance, frightens all parents.

"The suicide death of a loved one makes us reevaluate our own lives," said the sister of a young adult man who took his own life. "I fainted when I first heard about it. I kept thinking it was a joke. Sometimes I think it still hasn't happened."

Suicide is simply not in our frame of reference. Yet, whenever it's mentioned it becomes evident that all are touched by this tragedy.

Everyone seems to have a suicide story. Often it's been kept buried for years because families don't feel comfortable discussing something that has, in the past, been such a taboo subject.

A contractor who was working on my house after a fire destroyed a bedroom asked me what I was writing. When I told him about this book, he stood in the doorway, head down and said, "My brother committed suicide."

Tears welled in the eyes of this former Marine, father of nine children, as he related the experience that had occurred more than ten years ago.

Before he continued his story, he apologized for his tears.

"We'd gone out drinking together after work, and I always wondered if we hadn't done that, [if] he might still be alive. He had a drinking problem..."

My daughter called crying one day. "Mom, what can we do? Paula just committed suicide."

Paula worked in a medical office near my daughter's place of employment. Paula had previously asked one of the other workers to teach her how to give injections. The co-worker complied and a few days later, Paula gave herself a fatal drug injection. She left two children.

Not only has Paula left family and friends to grieve without the anchor of clearly knowing why she died, but the co-worker is left with the guilt that somehow, if she hadn't shown her how to give injections, Paula might still be alive.

The co-worker won't be alone, however. Paula's family and friends will most likely conjure up their own feelings of guilt, despite the knowledge that once the deed is done, no one else is responsible but the suicide victim.

One father whom I interviewed about the death of his young son was particularly open about his overwhelming feelings of grief, and acknowledged that men have a tougher battle dealing with the suicide of a loved one because they have been taught to contain their emotions.

I told him about another father who had stated flatly, "It doesn't bother me that much. I felt no guilt."

"He's lying," was the first father's comment.

Another survivor, who worked at a suicide prevention center, mentioned her work during a social occasion and a man at the table said, "Oh, my father committed suicide."

His wife's head spun around and she said, "You've never said that to anyone outside the family!"

Sometimes, however, it is more difficult to talk about it to family members. Janet B., whose brother committed suicide, avoided talking to her father about it for more than three years.

"I was afraid it would upset him," she says. But during a trip East when she called her father to let him know the plane was taking off, she confided to him, "I just want you to know that what happened to Mike wasn't your fault." Janet recalls there was a long silence on the other end of the telephone and then her father replied, "Well, I worked that out a long time ago and I know it wasn't." There was another long pause and then in a little voice her father asked, "How do you know it wasn't my fault?"

Janet acknowledges that she still wants to defend her brother, and defend her family. Once when giving a speech about her brother to raise money for a research grant, she realized most of it was a defense of her brother. "I felt the need to say my brother wasn't crazy. He wasn't on drugs and he hadn't been a failure. I wanted to tell them what a good family we came from."

Her story emphasizes why we're often shocked over many suicides. They don't fit anticipated patterns. Some people have lives filled with horror and they go on. Others seemingly have wonderful lives, and they end them in suicide.

Often when suicide is mentioned, people will at first shake their heads and say something like, "It's never touched my life." Then on reflection, they might add, "Come to think of it, I had an aunt who committed suicide, but no one ever talked about it," or, "I had a neighbor who shot himself, but it never affected me."

The truth is few of us will escape the shadow of suicide's touch. We can choose to ignore it, or we can grasp the emotions to our bosom in order to feel the deep grief and sorrow which, perhaps, make us more fully alive.

It is normal to grieve.

Psychotherapist Paul Hilsdale, shared with me part of a letter that he wrote to a grieving family whose son had committed suicide:

> "The element of suicide, I know, distorts your suffering, making it even more unbearable. How you must be blaming yourselves for his action. As a psychotherapist, I'm constantly reminded of the destructive power of guilt. And as a Buddhist-Christian, I know that one of our lifelong tasks is the gradual elimination of judgment (and self-condemnation). The jewel-self, the diamond that we were each given at birth seems to need such a final polishing — a cleansing away of judgment, till *what is* shines through the dust of what we would want to be.

"Recently I came across a poem by Rexroth, describing his reaction to the death of his wife, Andree. It begins: 'My sorrow is so wide/ I cannot see across it;/ And so deep I shall never/ Reach the bottom of it.' I would not want to take from you that sense of immensity and finitude — for your feelings are part of your essential diamond and rainbow. So I write with no expectation of mending your broken hearts, but only to let you know that you have understanding and caring companions way out here in California."

Although the stages of grief vary in intensity and don't always follow in a particular order, it is normal to have feelings of anger and rage when someone takes his or her own life. These same feelings also present themselves when death is by natural or accidental causes.

I remember attending a grief support group for widows and widowers one time as a reporter. One woman who arrived late said the minute she arrived, "I don't know why I'm here. It's depressing to be around all these sad people."

She proceeded to add, "My husband died only last week, and maybe I'm not ready for this."

She sat a few moments listening to some of the other people, jumped up, headed for the door and shouted, "None of you have problems like me. My husband left me with everything to do, and I don't know how to do any of it. I wish he were here just so I could scream at him for the fix he left me in."

After her outburst she left.

The group leader then asked how many had felt anger when their spouses died. All the participants raised their hands.

None of the deceased had committed suicide. Rather, they had died of natural causes, prolonged illnesses, or accidents. It's important to realize that the survivors of suicide go through the grieving process in similar fashion to those who lose loved ones from other causes.

Additionally, researchers are finding that survivors of suicide recover in similar ways to the survivors of any sort of death of a loved one. Most suicide survivors can't be distinguished from these other survivors two to four years after the death of a loved one.

Terrence Barrett, a counseling psychologist and instructor at Moorhead State University in Minnesota says that survivors of suicide may initially be stricken with more intense types of grief reaction, but ultimately they recover just as rapidly as do the bereaved in other types of death.

"Any death that occurs other than by natural means, such as an accident, adds to a survivor's grief," says Barrett.

Nor is there significantly more guilt among suicide survivors, he says. There may be greater feelings of anger because the person has taken his or her own life, but other forms of death also create anger.

The parents of a child who commits suicide will often direct their anger at others — an ex-spouse, other relatives, the authorities. "They are very hesitant to say they are angry at a son or daughter whereas, the spouse of someone who commits suicide becomes very angry at the deceased partner," says Barrett.

Survivors of suicide may try to spend more time by themselves, and probably will avoid people who bring up intense reactions in them. "For example, if someone is blaming them for the death, they will avoid that person. They are often sensitive to what other people have to say."

They are particularly sensitive to people who give their own interpretations without having the facts of the deceased person's life; to people who point blame; and to those who ask whether the person left a note and what it said.

But other survivors, as in the case of an accidental death, are also assaulted by insensitive people with remarks such as, "This might not have happened if you had been there."

"These other survivors [of a non-suicide] don't generally encounter the insensitivity of others to the degree suicide survivors do," says Barrett. But if, for instance, they had a fight with their loved one before an accidental death, they have similar feelings of guilt and heightened sensitivity to the comments of others. This sense of "unfinished business" is a common reaction to any unexpected death.

Researcher Jan van der Wal, M.D. of Leiden University in the Netherlands, who has also studied the grief reactions of suicide survivors says, "The most remarkable conclusion from our study is that the general assumption of pathology and extreme distress in survivors of suicide is not well founded."

"The assumption that suicide generally has devastating consequences for survivors, finds no support in our findings. Contrary to the suggestion that suicide is the most stressful cause of death, we found that traffic fatalities cause even more difficulties with detachment from the deceased than suicides."

He also says that suicide doesn't lead to a relatively complicated process of social adjustment, although he adds that the research isn't meant to minimize the severity of bereavement. It just shouldn't be exaggerated in the case of suicide. He says an expectation that suicide should provide more devastating effects than other forms of death can lead survivors to worry unnecessarily. It can also cause caregivers to become overanxious.

Van der Wal's emphasis is: If society expects a suicide survivor to be more devastated than survivors of other forms of death, it becomes a "self-fulfilling prophecy."

Adina Wrobleski of Minnesota, one of the nation's top suicidologists, says that the greatest need of survivors is reassurance that what they are going through is normal. Some of what they go through may be slightly different than that caused by other forms of death, such as thoughts of their own suicide, but it has nothing to do with the length of time it takes to recover.

Wrobleski began her studies on suicide following the death of her stepdaughter who shot and killed herself.

In her extensive research she has found that most survivors of suicide have trouble concentrating, a majority have sleeping difficulties, and that they feel guilty, angry and often dream of the deceased.

People suffering other types of bereavement often have some of these same symptoms, according to mental health professionals.

A majority of survivors of suicide, (as well as some who are grieving over other types of deaths) have also seen the death scene in their minds, have worried that someone else would die, thought they saw the person who died and have forgotten for a moment that the person was dead.

Grieving people of all sorts have panic attacks, headaches, stomach aches and back pain.

Survivors of suicide, however, sometimes have fleeting thoughts of their own suicide, or worry that others in the family will get a mental illness.

Wrobleski writes in the journal *OMEGA*, "there are many fears experienced by suicide survivors. I think the trauma of suicide death forces people to a vivid consciousness of their own death and the potential of everyone's suicide death. Because they are not really suicidal, these fleeting thoughts are frightening and are examples of the 'crazy' thoughts one can have. Another is the fear of mental illness once it has occurred in the family. Still another fear is an apprehension that 'someone else will die.'"

Carol V., a Nevada writer and mother, said she has periodically worried that she might be suicidal like her sister who took her own life at the age of thirty-five. She not only worries about herself, but has become concerned about her six-year-old daughter. She wonders if, perhaps, her daughter has inherited characteristics that might predispose her to problems that lead to suicide.

Many in the mental health profession believe there can be a genetic predisposition to illnesses, including severe depression, schizophrenia and manic-depression, that enhance the risk for suicide.

The National Institute of Mental Health states that depression can be associated with biological disturbances, possibly including genetic factors that may predispose some people to depression and suicide.

So studies in suicide are centering both on the suicide victim and the survivors, with a wealth of information that might help survivors understand their perplexing questions.

Carol V. acknowledges that in her mind, she's never laid her sister to rest, and that may contribute to her apprehension.

Eileen Simpson, a New York psychotherapist and author of *Orphans, Real and Imaginary,* lost her mother when she was one year old and her father when she was seven. She writes about how she didn't come to terms with it until she was middle-aged, following the death of her second husband of twenty years. She says that by not grieving properly over her mother's death, she prolonged her grief over her husband's death.

It isn't only adults who experience the grief process. Many times, surviving children are neglected following the death of a loved one. It has often been assumed that children don't feel grief with the same intensity and understanding as do adults.

Children do mourn, but perhaps in a different way, one that has been overlooked, according to Christina Sekaer, M.D., psychiatrist at St. Luke's Hospital of the St. Luke's Roosevelt Hospital Center in New York.

Sekaer writes in the *American Journal of Psychotherapy* that a redefinition of mourning specific to children of each age is needed, since many researchers believe children lack the ego strength and development to tolerate intense pain, and therefore cannot carry out the work of mourning.

She says that in order for children to mourn they need adult help to understand "the fact" of a death and to correct their misunderstandings as they develop. The child, even with adult help, cannot understand reality beyond his or her cognitive level.

The child may say, "Mommy's gone to heaven," but may not understand the finality of death. They may distort the event, according to Sekaer.

Children are particularly susceptible to feeling shame when returning to school after the suicide of a loved one, which means that they may need additional help in dealing with the grieving process, rather than being shunted aside in the belief that they don't understand what has happened.

We all need to grieve over losses in order for healing to take place.

Dana Brookins recalls that when her friend's twenty-six-year-old son committed suicide, the mother would sit downstairs in her two-story condominium and talk for a few minutes, and then excuse herself.

She would go upstairs and Dana could hear her pacing back-and-forth wailing as she had never heard any-one do before. "She would return anywhere from fifteen minutes to an hour later and sit down and talk a little more," and then she would excuse herself and go through the same process.

This open expression of grief is one key to grief recovery, as the following story indicates.

Jean M. shared her feelings with me less than a year after her son committed suicide:

"It's just sort of the ultimate. You worry about your kids getting home safely in a car. You're so happy when they reach eighteen. All your life, as parents, you learn not to hang onto your kids. You want them to survive.

"You sort of rationalize, and everyone says you did what you could. But in your heart, you can think of a lot of things that maybe you should have done and you felt, after all, you raised a child so that you wouldn't take care of it forever. You raise them to be able to get out of the nest and take care of themselves.

"And this [the suicide] is the ultimate failure."

Jean realizes she will have periods of mourning for her son the rest of her life. It has eased with time, but the pain will be with her always just as it is for anyone who loses a son or daughter to any form of death.

I'm recounting her story here in some detail because she was able to face her son's suicide immediately, and has gone on to enrich her own life immeasurably.

I refer to it as the "Blue Blanket" story, because it symbolizes the grieving process.

Jean is a single mother of three grown children including the son who committed suicide at the age of twenty-six following a successful concert tour in the Soviet Union and Asia with the musical group, "Hiroshima."

About midnight her former husband, a judge, called her at home in a California seaside town, about eighty miles from where he lived. He asked that she get a friend or neighbor to come over immediately and stay with her until he could get there. Then he told her over the phone that the police had just notified him of their son's suicide.

From the moment of the telephone call and through

the next two weeks, Jean was kept busy making arrangements, dealing with and responding to friends and acquaintances. "Those were the easiest times because I was busy all the time.

"You are in such a state of shock and there are things to do, like getting ready for the service. You're sort of insulated. It's later, when it all sinks in...when the insulation wears off...

"I was warned about this and it helped. A friend whose daughter had died suddenly of appendicitis told me, 'This is a piece of cake compared to what you're going to go through later.' It wasn't a cruel thing she told me. The love was just pouring out. And it helped."

As predicted, a week later Jan was lying on the bathroom floor or in the hall crying. "I'm glad I was warned," she said.

Since the suicide was reported in the papers, strangers responded with sympathy, she recalled. At no time did she ever consider hiding the fact that her son had committed suicide. "It didn't bother me to have it reported."

"We have to accept a certain amount of rottenness in life, and then go on from there," she said. Jean credits that attitude, plus the fact that she can cry a lot without feeling guilty, to helping pull her through.

Friends and family did the rest. Whenever she returned home she found that friends had filled the house with fresh fruit and flowers.

One evening a friend presented Jean with a soft, puffy, blue comforter. "I thought this might help keep you warm when you're feeling down," the friend said.

From that day on Jean used the blue blanket to snuggle up in whenever she was depressed — and she cried.

"It was quite bad at first. I cried for days. And it helped. But I still need to do that. I still cry. I haven't cried for a couple of weeks, but something small may happen and then

I cry. It's uncanny how the pain can be almost as sharp now when I get in one of the crying fits. It's such total grief that it's as bad as it was two weeks after his death.

"It doesn't happen as often or as long, but it was an enormous type of grief — the wracking of the body. I don't see how it could be any worse."

Jean would take the blanket to the bedroom or the closet or the bathroom and just lie on the floor with the lights out in the fetal position with the blanket over her head.

She knew instinctively it was good for her, she said.

"It's just something that my body and my mind and my emotions need to express. I think it's been helpful."

To fight the whirlwind of depression that can encircle the grieving, Jean's friends encouraged her to exercise. She recalled that one of her daughters literally forced her to go swimming every day.

The swimming, walking and running may have helped relieve some of Jean's depression. Neurophysiological studies indicate a tendency for a depressed person to have inappropriate levels of certain chemicals (such as serotonin and norepinephrine) in the brain that affect the neurotransmission of electrochemical signals from one brain nerve cell to another. These signals affect thoughts, behavior, feelings and emotions. Exercise temporarily alters the chemical balance in a positive way. The exercise need not be strenuous like running or jogging. Long walks can help.

Survivors frequently suffer various degrees of depression and some may need the aid of a psychiatrist or therapist and the administration of medication.

Jean said she went to a therapist twice, and took medication for a brief period of time.

Some mental health professionals believe that depression is a natural part of grief, and that if it isn't experienced, the person is simply repressing it. This short-lived depressive state, however, normally doesn't develop into a major depressive illness.

For those who repress their grief, it frequently comes out later in the form of physical illness.

Survivors of suicide may have fleeting thoughts of suicide themselves. These thoughts are a natural result of grief and of the fact that suicide has been introduced into their own frame of reference where it hadn't been before. In some cases however, the survivor may also have a genetic predisposition to depression and suicide.

Studies thus far are inconclusive as to why other family members think more about suicide after the death by suicide of a loved one.

Janet B., mentioned earlier, believes that suicide in a family opens doors that are best left closed. "I had this feeling for two years, before I started to talk about it — I'm Italian and German and I have a temper, and I slam doors and stuff — and I was terrified that in one of these fits of temper I was going to run out and buy a gun and shoot myself because my brother did.

"That's one of the reasons why I wanted to get a support group started, because I believe that 'post-vention' can be prevention too. Because once there is a suicide in the family people are more vulnerable once it's been introduced into their frame of reference."

Jean says she never thought of committing suicide, but that she did wish a couple of times that she would never ever wake up again.

"When I went to bed at night I had the two-button stage. One button would say, 'You're going to have to wake up and face the world in the morning,' and the other button would say that 'You're never going to have to wake up again.' I think at that time I would have pushed the never-wake-up button."

Jean talks about the double guilt she now carries because she's beginning to again enjoy life.

"There's a guilt about what you have failed to give the person. Some sense of reality that you failed to give him. And then also, you do feel a little guilty about enjoying your life. Because you allowed this awful thing to happen to your son you shouldn't be able to enjoy your own life.

"You have to live with the fact of ambivalence in your thinking that it might not be your fault. When I was first coming out into the real world again, I was able to be with people and enjoy myself. But at the same time, I would come home and cry and cry. I couldn't reconcile the two emotions. I remember saying to my daughter that one of them had to be false. Either when I'm out having a good time, it's phoney, because I'm really grieving. And when I was grieving, I'd say, 'What about the time I was out having a good time?' They're both real. What you're trying to do is to survive. You have very conflicting answers that come to you. And you get very depressed yourself. There is so much going wrong and it is so hard to survive. Life is that way. But you don't entirely believe it. And yet, the minute you start thinking about all that beauty out there, and you go and have a wonderful walk and everything is so glorious — then that is depressing too because it is all denied that person you love — that person who wasn't able to balance his life.

"It's too much to grasp. I don't think ever in my life I will be able to understand it. It is fruitless. You really want to know what happened. But you know you never will. He had so much promise. Was so kind. And was so miserable."

Adina Wrobleski writes in her newsletter that the guilt survivors feel when they start to enjoy life again is called "recovery guilt," and she offers the following quote from the journal *OMEGA:*

"Recovery guilt occurs long after the [person's] death, when the [survivors] begin to feel better, to enjoy life, and to resume living without so much focus and energy going into the grief process. Recovery guilt is a sense that one is violating a standard because one can again laugh, relax, and enjoy life even though one's [loved one] has died."

Jean wonders if she will ever get over the occasional thought that her son took his life because she was a bad mother. It's as if, on some level, there is an instinctual assumption that she must have been bad or he wouldn't have died. There are moments when she wonders if other people believe she was a bad mother.

"You sort of feel stamped as a failure as a parent. But that's in your mind. I never got that from anyone else."

Mary S. Cerney, a psychologist at the Menninger Foundation, says survivors of suicide go through much more guilt than the average grieving person. They wonder how they have contributed to the suicide, and they often think society will blame them. As van der Wal pointed out, this could be a self-fulfilling prophecy, because it's expected, rather than a reality.

Whatever the cause of this guilt, most survivors have it in one form or another. "Guilt. That's the biggie. I still have it. At least I can help some people now because I couldn't help my brother. I still believe that if he had said something, and we could have gotten him through the next month, maybe he wouldn't have killed himself," says Janet B.

In talking with other survivors — sisters, brothers, friends, mothers, fathers, spouses — they all occasionally ask the question, "Was I somehow to blame because I was a bad mother, father, sister, brother, friend, or spouse?"

To a degree, we're all responsible, individually and as a society for what happens to our fellow brothers and sisters. But that doesn't mean we personally have to accept blame.

Even those who should be trained to help sometimes can't resist placing blame. One such person is a specialist in childhood suicide and depression.

After I recounted the death of Jean's son he remarked, "Well, obviously, it was the parent's fault."

"When a child commits suicide, it's the parent's fault," he reiterated.

Stunned, I argued that the son was twenty-six years old and had been close to his parents. I proceeded to tell him about how the father had taken his vacation one summer with his son after the youth had come home at about age sixteen and said he wanted to hitchhike to San Francisco. The father, a very dignified-looking judge said, "Okay, but I'm going with you." The two hitchhiked the more than nine hundred miles round trip together.

The psychologist backed off and placed blame on the fact that the youth was a musician. "They're all kind of strange," he said.

Though disenchanted with this particular psychologist, I then explained how the son was a serious musician from a musical family. "Does this doom someone?" I asked.

He backed off again and said that perhaps the youth was mixed up in drugs, or was a homosexual or was despondent over a bad love affair, which he said are all possible contributing factors to suicide, although these conditions aren't the actual "cause" of a suicide.

At no time did this particular psychologist show the slightest sympathy, love, understanding or humility that most professionals exhibit.

When seeking professional help if and when it's needed, look around and don't feel you have to stay with the first counselor or therapist you find.

Dana, a friend who heard of my disenchantment with the psychologist who wanted to place blame, is a published and award-winning children's book author. She wrote me a note saying, "When anyone starts casting blame for suicide, he/she had better look in all directions. A friend of mine, a homosexual, was just shot and killed last week in a boxcar.

Whose fault was that? His parents, the environment, society, his genes, the transient (a former mental patient) who shot him? I think all of them were responsible.

"What parent among us can cast the first stone?

"There's very little room for the fragile ones in our society, the ones who need to be held up more than people can hold them up. Sure, the parents had some part in it. So did Oswald, and Nixon or Von Braun and the first guy who ever owned a slave. We just don't have much room in this society or tolerance for our butterflies."

Survivors don't need to be judged when a catastrophe like suicide enters their lives.

They need the support of people who give them blue blankets. They need people — non-judgmental friends — because they're not dealing in theories. They don't have the luxury of speculating on why the person killed him or herself. The deed has already been done. They are dealing with instant pain. Pain that begins the moment they receive the telephone call or discover the body; pain that will stay with them in some small portion of their hearts for the rest of their lives.

This pain, however, can engulf anyone who loses a loved one, regardless of the cause of death.

Tears still occasionally come into the eyes of a friend who lost a son, a policeman, in the line of duty ten years ago; to a woman whose husband was killed in World War II; to a mother whose child died at birth twelve years ago.

Grief is a natural part of life, and therefore not one to smother. It can be carried in small places of the heart after the initial grieving period. Only when it becomes the central focus of the life, long after the death, is it unhealthy, and then professional help to lay it to rest may be necessary.

"Great grief makes sacred those upon whom its hand is laid. — Joy may elevate, ambition glorify, but only sorrow can consecrate," wrote Horace Greely.

And Sir Aubrey de Vere, an 18th century poet wrote, "Grief should be like joy, majestic, sedate, confirming, cleansing, equable, making free, strong to consume small trouble, to command great thought, grave thought, thoughts lasting to the end."

Although you may feel that you want to be alone, it often helps to allow others to share the grief.

Looking back, Jean said she'll never forget the help given her by family and friends. But she believes that the survivors, as well, can help those who are supporting them.

"As a survivor, you must know that it may be difficult for some of your friends to know what to do," she notes.

"You must know how impotent your friends feel. You must realize that they don't know what to do. It's awkward for them. And you don't mind. You try to put them at ease and help them because they're trying to imagine what you're going through. But they can't quite imagine how awful it is. But they can come close.

"Popping in on people [the survivors] is okay. And calling, although sometimes I didn't answer. But I had the choice. Sometimes it would be 3:00 PM., in the middle of the afternoon, and I would have my robe on. And I wouldn't want to answer the door, but I did. And it was someone who said, 'Let's go take a walk on the beach'. Or 'Let's do this'...and it helped.

"I don't know how you can instruct people to be that sensitive. My friends just seemed to know. Just leave it up to the bereaved person and take a clue from them. Don't push a discussion. My friends were so accepting of my moods. Accepting and helpful."

Eventually, Jean realized she had to get on with life. "You have to get in a situation where your mind is on something else — the mechanics of living — perhaps a job. You have to be distracted from this thing that happened. If you just sit and think about the horror of it, you would be gone.

"I didn't think I would ever go back to the choral [a group she had recently joined]. How could I walk into that room? They all knew. Four months later, my daughter talked me into going. I liked singing and they were all nice to me. After I got there, I just barely made it through the evening. I didn't think it was going to be a bummer, but it was. I said I'd never go back. But my daughter made me go back and it became easier."

Jean persisted and now says it's something she really enjoys. "Don't be surprised if something you think is going to be easy and good turns out to be difficult."

Now, several years later, Jean says that she still gets sad and weeps occasionally thinking about her son's suicide. Pain is a stranger to none of us, and we all need blue blankets of one sort or another.

Janet B., whom I mentioned earlier, acknowledges that even several years after her brother's death she still grieves and sometimes feels irrational guilt about her brother. "He was a very gentle person, even as a child. He was afraid of moths and I used to catch them and toss them in his face. Sometimes I wonder, and I know it's silly, but I wonder if that could have contributed to his taking his life," she says.

Suicide expert Dr. Mamoru Iga, also a specialist in Japanese culture, says the Japanese think any death is natural. "To them, suicide is bad, but they don't take it so hard. Americans have an unenlightened view of death and should learn to get on with life.

"Japanese don't have the conception of Hell. They have the family altar — Butsudan — where remaining family members communicate with the dead. They can ask help from the suicide victim. Americans are afraid of death because they lose complete communication, but not the Japanese," says Dr. Iga.

Because many Japanese are, in a sense, in touch with their ancestors, they handle their grief by talking to them about why they committed suicide. And they share their feelings of how it affected them. "They speak to them with love," says Iga. "This allows them to settle accounts with the deceased and to get on with their own lives."

Western culture is adopting some of these methods.

Cerney, the Menninger psychologist who specializes in dealing with grieving patients, uses a method similar to Eastern tradition.

Working with a process she calls "imaging," in which the patient relaxes and envisions a real past event or an imagined scene in their minds, she encourages her patients to "image" the deceased and to speak with them. "I continually emphasize for them not to put words into the person's mouth. I believe the grieving person really knows the answers, but this helps bring it out.

"If they feel they have done something wrong to contribute to the person's suicide, they ask the deceased to forgive them. But first we must get rid of the anger. They are usually angry that the person could cop out on life — like a wife who is left with the burden and little income.

"We have to get them to accept or understand the person and why they did it, and they have to forgive them. The big issue is letting go. Then they are on a different level — acceptance.

"The survivors have limitations. They can't be responsible for others all the time. Maybe they did make some mistakes," she says, but they shouldn't feel responsible for their loved one's suicide.

"One of the biggest problems is that they don't get social support because suicide isn't acceptable."

Success of the therapy depends on how long they have been grieving and how much knowledge they have about suicide, according to Cerney.

Therapy usually involves two or three sessions after being referred to her by the client's regular therapist.

"Some have been grieving for twenty or thirty years, and they all wish they had come sooner. Sometimes it's easier with long-term grievers. By that time, they've had other losses, and they know what loss is.

"But this isn't quick magic. It depends on the individual. Some people can't use it. Those who use [the suicide] as a badge of courage, and have lived their lives as a martyr, don't really want to get over it. Their lives revolve around the grieving. But if people want to get over it and get on with life, they will."

Cerney began using her methods several years ago, and said she learned them from her patients.

When she had patients under hypnosis and asked them to return to the origin of the difficulty that had brought them into treatment, they would frequently return to "unfinished business" connected with a loss. Other patients came who seemed unable to pass through the mourning process and get on with their lives.

She dropped the hypnotism when she realized more people were comfortable with imaging instead. "Perhaps imagery's main contribution in grief work is that it allows the individual an opportunity to handle unfinished business with the deceased. Feelings not expressed before can now be expressed, misunderstandings can be clarified, and memories can be healed.

"Some patients, however, can't let go because the deceased has become an integral part of their sense of self. For them to let go would mean a loss of identity, a disintegration of the self. On some occasions, when I think the patient has worked through all the necessary issues but the deceased individual still has not left, I may ask the patient what would permit them to let go."

Following the "letting go" patients report a sense of lightness and freedom, says Cerney. "They are very tired as though they have let go of a very heavy burden," she says.

Many people are able to work through their grief without professional help, but no one need be ashamed or feel guilt if they need help in letting go of the burden.

"There is a separate question of whether suicide survivors need therapy or support," writes Wrobleski in the journal *OMEGA*. "The answer, I believe, is that most need support, some need therapy, and some need both. In the sparse literature there is on survivors, I think there is often an assumption that suicide bereavement is so traumatic an event that some form of treatment is automatically necessary. Grief, however, is not an illness or disorder but a natural part of life, and consequently, most people just need support and help through the grieving process."

Edwin Shneidman, a noted suicide expert, writes in *Suicide & Life-Threatening Behavior*, "With humans ... this grief process ... takes about a year. But, of course, the figurative sands of secondary grief stay on the beaches of our psyches all the remainder of our lives."

2

SURVIVORS SPEAK OUT

THE FOLLOWING poem was written by David Hoffman, now a law student, shortly after his brother Dean committed suicide in 1985 at the age of twenty-one.

This Ain't No Nightmare

I saw him laying there,
    (a nightmare come true)
In a coffin.

Oh! Brother of mine...why?

Bleary, teary-eyed,
I gazed at him,
    refracting his image through salty eyes.
    His reflections running down my cheeks,
    collecting swiftly in a pool on the floor.
Worse — even — than the sight, was the sound.

His silence was deafening (or is it Death-ening?),
But my wailing, and my family's (and friends)
Overwhelmed my senses,

cracked our foundations,
rattled our reality of our world.

There is no sense in suicide!

Only pain.
    Pain which grounds us.
    Pain which awakens us.
    Pain which lets us know this ain't no nightmare.
'Cause you can wake up from a nightmare feeling safe
    and sane.
We are disoriented; in pain.

Nope, this ain't no nightmare.
    We can't roll over, go back to sleep and wake up again,
    feeling safe and refreshed, secure in our world, with
    just a hint of the adrenaline-flowing night-before in
    slightly damp sheets.
No. We awaken from soaking sheets, feeling less-secure,
    sicker full of that adrenaline's fight or flight
    feeling, knowing we can't do either. Knowing that the
    pain and misery and grief we feel is the only thing
    keeping us sane.

This ain't no nightmare, but I wish it was.

A MOTHER'S STORY

As a pediatric nurse and nursing instructor at Kaiser
Permanente Hospital in Redwood City, California, Yvonne
(Taffy) Hoffman has seen her share of dying children. She
has comforted the parents in their grief, but says nothing
prepared her for the suffering she experienced when her
son committed suicide.

"You deal with a lot of guilt and anger. I have the feeling that when I walk into a room people are saying, 'That's the mom of the boy who committed suicide.'"

And anger nearly overwhelms her when a well-meaning friend says something like, "At least you have four other children."

"I want to tell them that if I lost one of my fingers I'd want it back. That I lost a child and I want him back."

She lives with her husband, Saul, a mechanical engineer, and raised five children, including Dean, who killed himself in 1985 by jumping off a cliff.

Taffy recalls that she was especially angry at the psychologists who had treated Dean and failed to recognize the depth of his depression. And she got angry at friends who couldn't handle it — who shied away. "Once they just come forward and acknowledge and say they couldn't handle it, I'll feel better. Why do you suppose they shy away? I really think they don't know what to say. Part of it is that I don't have the energy to support them. It's really hard for them, I know."

"But there have been friends who were especially comforting and still are. "At first, our closest friends were with us, and they were helpful in that they just listened. People still call and say, 'We were just thinking of you,' and 'How are you feeling?' A lot of people remember that February is hard for us."

Anger returns when Taffy hears snide remarks from other staff at the hospital when an attempted suicide is admitted. "Oh, well, have to baby-sit this one," she hears.

The pain is intensified when she reads an article like one in a major publication about four kids in New Jersey who committed suicide. "They [the magazine] referred to them as losers — on drugs," she recalls.

"I get upset, too, when I read articles that try to place blame when a young person commits suicide, such as, 'He/

she did it because of lousy grades, or a breakup with a girlfriend or boyfriend.' What's that got to do with anything? There aren't simple reasons like that for someone committing suicide."

Taffy worries about her other children — the pain they are feeling, and she recalls that since Dean's death they have, at times, all climbed into bed together to hold one another as they used to when they were little.

Her husband, whom she describes as a former "macho man," has learned to weep and acknowledge pain and fear. "He's completely changed. He's much more into himself. He still gets uptight at different things, but reminds himself to calm down.

"Men don't have as many close friends as women. They don't have the support systems, but he's got one good friend who asks him 'How you doing?' and he knows he doesn't have to lie to him. He doesn't have to say, 'I'm feeling fine.'

"We game play. Each member of the family tries to protect the other. If I'm down, someone else tries to be up. Now we can acknowledge when we're down and that's okay. It's natural to game play, but it's important to be honest," she says.

Taffy has joined a support group, and the family has received some counseling. One particular counselor who had also lost a son was very helpful, she says.

One of her sons has joined a support group, "Survivors of Suicide," and he's ridden a two-hundred-mile bike-a-thon to raise money for a scholarship fund established in Dean's memory. Another son is putting his feelings into poetry. She and her husband help each other through their mood swings, and they're active in a local youth organization.

She talks about her lack of energy during the first few weeks of the tragedy. "Our rabbi made most of the arrangements. He helped us think. We could barely walk from room to room."

Nearly three hundred people attended the funeral, and a little bit of tradition was broken. "One of the conservative Jewish traditions is for each member of the family to shovel dirt into the grave site. Nearly everyone, including friends, took a turn and almost filled up the grave."

"It's powerful — the dirt. You are putting dirt over your own child.

"Life will never be the same, but then, life goes on," she says.

When new acquaintances ask how many children she has, Taffy usually answers, "Five."

"Then it gets harder when they ask what they're doing, and I go 'uh...' and then I have to tell them about Dean.

"Another interesting thing is when you start feeling good. You're almost frightened of it. It's the guilt. You start thinking, 'Oh my God, it's my son and I'm not feeling bad'. You're damned if you do, and damned if you don't," reflects Taffy.

"Just don't say it was God's will. None of this was God's will."

A WIFE'S PERSPECTIVE

Six months after her husband Richard's death from suicide, Diane C. is struggling to put her life back together again.

"It's just too big. I don't know any other word to describe it. Everyone has problems and you can talk them through and work them through and find solutions. There is no solution to death. It is so final. I mean, I can't ever go back. Can't ever recapture any moments. I don't have any control at all. I'm just powerless. I've never even had the word suicide in my vocabulary. I never understood the pain Richard felt until this happened," she says.

"It's too bad it's just a complicated subject, suicide. The person isn't around to explain. My husband and I were on a ten-day cruise and we came back on Sunday, and I found him dead on Tuesday. We had one of the most intimate, wonderful times of our lives on the cruise..."

"There were problems on the cruise, however. Richard, who was a psychologist, was recovering from the flu. He had missed two weeks of work, which was the only time in ten years, except for one other day, that he had missed work.

"We had planned this cruise — I had just finished an M.B.A. program, and the cruise was a sort of motivation for me — and it was to be a kind of rehabilitation for him.

"He was still dealing with the flu virus on the cruise and said he wanted to see the doctor. All of a sudden he was talking in terms of his depression, burnout and overwork. It was obvious to us that he needed some intense therapy. We talked about it a lot on the cruise and decided he would see a psychiatrist, and perhaps, go to a psychiatric unit."

On the Monday morning following the end of the trip they went to the family doctor, and he suggested a psychiatrist, who then recommended intense therapy. Richard chose to enter a hospital, and he was scheduled to go there Tuesday.

"I left for work that morning and came home that night and found him dead. He chose not to go to the hospital. He must have decided Monday night not to go because he left me a note that he'd apparently written Monday night. Sometime Tuesday morning he killed himself."

But Diane doesn't believe the suicide itself was something that happened overnight. "Now that it's over, I found a journal and he had been having problems for a long time. It wasn't something like us having a fight. Suicide doesn't happen like that. People who are suicidal are suicidal for a long time, although I don't believe he decided to do it until that evening. It may have been out there as an option before, but I think having to come to terms with it, as a therapist, and with himself, was the ultimate loss of control for him.

"Looking back I can see the signs of stress — the twitching in the eyes, his liver count was up, almost diabetic. Things were happening and we laughed it off because he was over forty. It wasn't until the cruise that we took it seriously. The doctor asked him if he was suicidal and he told the doctor he had thought of jumping overboard.

"Of course, he [Richard] was a psychologist, and he knew just what to say. He'd say, 'Yes, I had the thought, but I wouldn't act on it.' We all say things like that — 'I wish I was dead' — but we don't act on it. But I became concerned about his emotional well-being on the cruise. The psychiatrist said there was no way to have known. 'I see suicidal people all the time, and I didn't diagnose him as really being that way,' he said.

"Richard wasn't psychotic. He was like anybody else who has depression. But it was much more extreme than he ever let us know."

Diane describes the night she found him as the worst in the world. "I walked in and he was lying on the floor at the foot of the bed facing the opposite direction. I ran up to him, felt his leg and it was cold. I ran to the neighbors and they called the paramedics. They didn't try to save him. Rigor mortis had already set in. I called my family doctor and the paramedics called my sister."

The sister came immediately, but the rest of her family, and Richard's, were out of state and came later.

She doesn't remember much more of what happened, except that she first called at about 8:00 PM. but the paramedics, and the police did not leave until about 11:30

PM., right after the body was removed. "It was horrible."

"Thank God I had a church. My religious background was helpful," she says. The minister who had married them and who was a good friend was with her the next day. Richard had been meeting for about fifteen years to play poker with a group of graduates from the theological seminary where he had attended school, and the minister was part of that group.

"It really hurt those guys that Richard wasn't able to confide or share with them," she says.

Diane returned to work after two weeks, and now says she probably needed three. "That first week I mostly cried at work. In some ways, I thought it was good to get back to work, in terms of distraction. But in many other ways it just seemed like everything was so insignificant in comparison to my tragedy. Still, it was either that or stay home alone. The family had to go back to work, and it would have been worse staying in the house by myself. I didn't have anywhere else to go. I couldn't travel."

Upon returning to work, she found that most people were understanding, but would try to distract her rather than deal with the suicide. "Some people couldn't acknowledge his dying. That was worse than the people who came in and said, 'It must be really difficult,' and who allowed me to talk about it."

"There is a need for people to understand that I was a good wife. That I wasn't a nagging wife. That I wasn't the reason he killed himself. There was a need to let others know we had a good marriage and our relationship had nothing to do with him killing himself. There is a stigma about suicide. People don't know that it's more nurturing and more caring for someone to talk about it than for them to come in and start talking about the weather, or work. People don't understand the tragedy of this. They don't understand. They can't unless it has happened to them."

Diane believes that unless a person has been faced with such adversity, they may not know how to talk to the bereaved. "My boss had an aunt die after I went back to work, and I went into his office and let him know that if he just needed to talk I'd be there. I don't know if I would have been able to do that before Richard's death."

She joined a support group where she received the understanding she needed. "That's one of the things about support groups. I was able to validate some of my feelings — even some of the physical things I was going through.

"I was thirsty all the time. Didn't want to eat. Became dehydrated. I had diarrhea. And of course I had trouble sleeping. Shock causes things you have no control over".

Diane had to search for a suicide survivor's support group, and wishes there were more available so that all survivors could have ready access to the help they can provide. "A regular bereavement group is good, but it isn't the same as one for survivors," she says.

"Just talking with and hearing from people who have gone through the same thing helped. You are caught off guard. I think people are always caught off guard with suicide. You're always asking, 'What if?' Wondering what role you played, 'what if' you had done this, or that. There are just questions that will never be answered," she says.

Several things particularly helped Diane in the support group. One was that the survivors read the letters left by the suicide victim. "I want to show my letter, but who else wants to read it? But people who have gone through this know. We talked about what their face looked like. Or what their body felt like. It's unbelievable how interested they are in hearing other people's experiences. My letter was so long. He wrote twelve pages. It doesn't say much. It doesn't tell me why he killed himself, but it says good-bye. Most of the other letters were much more brief. But the similarity is that you can hear that they're in a lot of pain, and you can't understand why. He said he was really confused and mixed-up, and the best thing for him to do was leave. It's hard to imagine that. There had to have been a chemical imbalance. I don't believe my husband was rational at the time he killed himself.

"There are so many forms of depression. What's difficult about Richard's letter is that he is so controlled. If he hadn't talked about killing himself [in the letter] you wouldn't have diagnosed him as suicidal. He was so articulate."

Diane recalls that many of the other letters dealt with money problems. "My husband thought he had money problems. He was obsessed with it, even though he had a very successful practice. But he couldn't ever make enough. He made [the problem] out bigger than it really was."

The group also shared pictures of their loved ones, and that helped, she says.

"It's just important for other people to validate you. A man at my church told me it would take three or four years to get over the worst grief, and that helped me. I keep thinking it's been almost six months, and I think I have to hurry. So he gave me hope that I'm progressing and that I'm not hopeless. But everyone has a different time frame. It's like once the funeral is over, the show's over.

"The most comfortable time is the first two weeks. People come and cry with you. They want to hold you. People are around. The first time I had to stay by myself it was horrible."

Other help came from Diane's therapist, whom she had been seeing prior to the suicide. "There are so many people who don't witness or don't acknowledge, or can't acknowledge the tragedy and the pain when they lose someone this close. It's almost hard for anyone to conceptualize. My therapist was good at saying, 'That must really hurt,' or 'This is the most painful thing you will go through in your life.'

"My therapist says I should get a tee-shirt that says, 'I'm still in pain.'

"It doesn't help for someone to say, 'Go out to dinner and you'll feel better.' But when people say they understand how bad it feels, that really helps.

"I want to believe that it is the worst I will ever go through.

"It's a tragedy because it has totally changed my life. I had a life and now I don't have any. My husband was my life. The other things I do — my work and my school — were only secondary."

A friend talked her into getting a dog, a Sealyham Terrier. He took her to meet it, and she fell in love. "And it helped. I've never had a dog. He just saved my life. So many evenings I come home and I just live for this dog. It needs me, and I need something that needs me," says Diane.

"He's a wonderful dog. I've transferred so much caring from Richard onto him. It's amazing how much I'm attached to it."

"You can't realize until you lose your spouse how many things you don't know about yourself. You don't realize how many things you do because of your partner. All of a sudden you don't know what kind of furniture you like, what you like to watch on TV, or even if you like TV. It's just a tragedy that somebody I fantasized retiring with and growing old with, I'm never going to see again. I'm going to look at a picture of him when I'm sixty, and he'll still be forty-three."

Diane says she'd like to remarry someday. "I'm scared stiff of a relationship, but I know I want to get married again, and I think that's healthy. If people have a good marriage and lose that spouse, it's not unusual that they want to get married again. Still, I feel like I might be carrying so much garbage with me, so I don't know.

"If I ever get through it and to the other side and have another life, and I believe in my heart I will, I'm going to do whatever I can to help any other woman. No one should have to go through this, but they will. I'm thirty-five and no thirty-five-year-old woman should have to go through this. It's just too big of a tragedy.

"But who knows what I'm going to do. I know my life ahead is going to have a lot of changes — that I have to die and be reborn, that I'm not going to live the same life without Richard.

"Right now," she says, all she's concerned with is "getting through the day."

LOSS OF A MOTHER AND FATHER

Leslie Elliott is a metaphysical counselor living in the mountain community of Wrightwood, California, who vividly recalls the suicides of his mother and father more than thirty years ago.

The events shaped the entire course of his life.

"My father committed suicide when I was eleven and my mother committed suicide just after I turned eighteen, and I want to tell you, first of all, every suicide is a horror story, every one of them.

"It means that a person has obviously come to a point where they can't see beyond a certain wall. They feel there is no reason to go on living. None of us were consulted about coming into life. We were just brought here. We were brought here out of forces we had no control over."

"I always feel there is enough love and beauty [in the world] to anesthetize the pain [in our lives], but for some there isn't," he says.

"I've spent forty years thinking about this. [Suicide] is the anesthetic for this god-awful [life] we go through, especially for sensitive people."

Leslie recalls that when his father committed suicide

by hanging himself at his office during the lunch hour, he never gave any signs. "He never talked about it. There was no expectation."

Friends he was staying with in Wrightwood whom he had known since the age of five told him of the death, but not the circumstances. He found great strength from them through this first ordeal and others that beset him throughout his life.

In the 1940s, when Leslie was a young child, Wrightwood was a gathering place for some of the most noted metaphysical teachers and practitioners in the United States. Leslie was introduced to "their very fine minds."

Among them were Aldous Huxley and Dr. K.E. Mullendorf, the first woman ordained under Ernest Holmes of the Science of Mind Church.

It was Mullendorf who broke the news to him of his father's death.

"She asked me to come upstairs and the first thing she said was, 'How strong are you?' and I asked her 'Why?' She said she had something very serious to tell me. 'Your father died today.'

"She didn't tell me how he died, so the first shock was the news of his death. Suddenly you don't breathe. Everything just comes to a screeching halt. Death is so final in the sense that you never see that person again. I was silent. Speechless. If I had known him to be sick or disturbed, or hospitalized, it might have helped form coping mechanisms for the finality."

A Jewish rabbi and Mullendorf conducted the funeral, and then afterwards, Leslie discovered a letter his aunt had sent describing the details of his father's death.

"He was a pottery manufacturer with a large plant in Manhattan Beach, and he hung himself in the office during lunchtime. The staff found him. He'd been a World War I veteran and had been exposed to mustard gas. He apparently had a heart condition none of us knew anything about. In the letter, he said he was afraid he would be a burden to the family, but I think there was more to it. That was my introduction to suicide."

Leslie says that after his father's death the family fell apart because the relatives had never liked his mother, and they blamed her.

"She just couldn't stand the loneliness and isolation she must have felt. She had moments of feeling responsible. You can't escape feelings of guilt whether it is imagined or justified. You carry it the rest of your life. You never get over the feeling that this person has rejected you. 'What did I do wrong?' you think.

"I'm sure I had no direct reason to feel this, but I did.

"The thing that is so ironic in this situation is that people would say to me, 'People who talk about it never do it. Those who don't talk are the ones who do it'— wrong, wrong, wrong! My father never talked about it, and my mother never stopped talking about it until she did it."

At times she tried to talk her young son into committing suicide with her.

"I lived with the feeling that at any moment we were going to die. She was full of melancholy and at one time told me that when I graduated from high school, she would do it. When we were all teary eyed at graduation, I had the impression when the principal put the diploma in my hand that it was my mother's death certificate. Finally one day I told her, 'I know you're miserable, but I'm curious enough to want to go on and see what's around the corner.' I knew by this time I could deal with whatever I had to deal with."

Leslie realizes he didn't come out of the experience unfazed, however.

"I realized early on that I might never have a meaningful relationship. The residual feelings of rejection and distrust had stayed with me. 'Are they going to do the same thing? Am I going to get attached and then be left again?'"

Leslie, who was schooled in psychology, says, "There's another thing you go through the rest of your life. You have terrible feelings of pity for these people, but you are also very angry at them for leaving and rejecting you. That's a terrible ambivalence, but the anger is normal and healthy."

Just before his mother committed suicide, she quit talking about it and Leslie grew hopeful. "She was cheerful. We planned a trip. She felt very content. I thought she was coming out of it."

After graduation Leslie was sent to Wrightwood for a vacation. The last time he saw his mother was when she took him to the bus stop. When he returned home at the appointed time, she was supposed to meet him at the same bus stop but she never came.

"I got down to the Beverly Hills bus station and that's where I usually called her, but there was no answer. I thought maybe she was out for a walk and I waited, but then my heart started pounding and I knew it was the time I had dreaded for seven years. So I took another bus and got off and started walking up hills to the house carrying my suitcase. Something told me, 'Be ready now.'"

As Leslie neared his home he noticed three days of newspapers lying on the lawn. He opened the door and smelled a terrific odor and then noticed his mother's body by the oven.

Leslie called a neighbor and after that, "Everything became a blur. I remember cops, the fire department...it was like I was in a state of suspended animation. It was a scene all built out of wax. From that time forward, I've never believed much in life. Something in me died and I've never come out of it."

When I asked Leslie what kept him going, and why and how he continues to help so many people, he says, "As far as I know, one thing stands out. These people have met an end to their suffering. I get very irate when I hear amateur counselors say, 'You're never given more of a burden than you can carry.' That's out and out bull. We're given horrible things. I look at life as a jungle war, but still have rose-colored glasses."

Other things that anger him are when people who believe in reincarnation say "without any sensitivity" that whoever commits suicide will have to come back and live it all over again, and religious fundamentalists that "tell you you're going to burn in Hell if you commit suicide."

"Can you imagine suffering through a loved one's death and then thinking they're going to have to come back and do all that misery again? No human being has a right to impose that terrible thought on another who has suffered and gone through the terrible pain of seeing people who couldn't cope in this terrible life end it."

Leslie believes that he's fortunate to have been introduced to metaphysical teaching and the loving friends he made along the way.

"Somewhere along the line, I could have taken a bottle of pills, but I feel there has been an investment made in me, and I should respect this.

"It takes more courage to live than to die. If we're here to go through this, we're obviously here to develop some kind of understanding and maybe pass it on to someone else. I came to a point in my life that I said, 'If I'm here, it's for a reason. I'm not interested in me. I'm interested in feeling good. If I can get a good night's sleep, good food and a pleasant walk...'"

He tells me this as he gazes out the window of his cabin in the mountains where tall pines grow. Some are dropping their cones to the ground, and a blue jay is pecking at one of them. Leslie smiles.

Turning back to me he recalls a time when he became utterly depressed and was complaining to a woman he'd met who had been through the Holocaust. "She slapped me and said, 'I want you to remember this all your life. Suffering is normal.'"

A WORRIED FATHER

Jack Simonson is the father of three sons, now in their late twenties and early thirties. His life was touched three times within the same year in the early eighties when three different friends of his each had a son commit suicide.

He was so shaken by the events that he composed a letter to his sons, one of whom is paralyzed from a wrestling accident that occurred in high school.

"I think I wrote the letter out of pure fear...plain and simple," he says.

"So many of the kids from that generation (the late sixties) were messed up, including my own kids. They were just sort of wandering. They were raised to make their own decisions at an early age and that was pretty confusing to them. They just couldn't put a price on life.

"I remember Jay came home from high school one day and the teacher had asked him what he wanted to learn. The teacher had said, 'What do you want to learn in science?' They didn't want to learn anything. They didn't want to be in school to begin with. That's a terrible burden to place on kids."

In retrospect Simonson said the generation of the late sixties was also taught to question everything.

Those thoughts were on his mind when the suicides began hitting close to home. "It's so easy to lose track of these kids. We taught them to solve problems on their own. So that got me started thinking of the possibility of one of my own kids doing the same thing.

"I felt comfortable that we had a good, open relationship, and then I thought, 'Do we really?'

"Then a couple more things happened. There was a plane wreck at Rialto Municipal Airport. Two passengers sitting side by side. One guy walked away from it, and the other who was sitting just a few inches away from him died — speared by a piece of metal."

Simonson says his thought was, "If you don't tell your kids that you love them, if you don't make it clear to them, maybe you won't have enough time. I just felt that I had never really told my kids I loved them."

In the letter to his three sons he wrote that, "Life is a matter of inches and seconds."

"Everything happens so fast," he says. "You don't really get a chance to tell them you love them. It's too late when they're in a casket or are hanging from the rafter.

"Basically I just told them I loved them very much and if they ever had any problems, that before they attempted to do anything on their own, or to commit suicide, to talk to me first...*please.*

"I talked openly to them about the possibility of committing suicide. That probably everyone thinks of it. That it's a problem you can't solve by yourself. That you need help with it."

He also told them that, "Those who are left after the incident are the ones who suffer the most, so that it wasn't fair not to at least give us a chance to talk to them."

Simonson acknowledges that he was raised in a generation that was taught not to show emotion. "I think our generation and the one before was like that. My dad was a physician and I never saw him...very seldom. And he never said he loved me.

"And that's the way I was raised — that it wasn't a manly thing to do. You don't hug your kids. My kids weren't raised much different, but I hug them now. It wasn't easy at first, because they'd never had it before."

Simonson believes that since the ice has been broken,

he and his sons are much closer. "It's the best of times," he says.

"Of all the kids who have a right to do something like that, Kurt is the one. And I think he is too strong to do it. I don't think any of my kids would do it, but then, the drunkard is the last one to think he's an alcoholic.

"That's the problem. You really never know."

Simonson believes that his son Kurt's accident, that left him paralyzed, taught him that bad things do happen to good people.

But he also remembers a time when Kurt talked about suicide.

"I can tell you, I can remember that just like it was yesterday. He was lying in bed. He had very limited movement, and he said, 'I wish I was dead.'

"It made me so angry that I chewed him out something fierce. If I could have picked him up I would have shook him. I told him that not being alive was not acceptable and that I never wanted to hear him talk like that again.

"He's accepted it, even though he doesn't like it. He's still hopeful that something out there will help him. He's worked hard at surviving, so I don't think he ever would [attempt suicide].

"Maybe Kurt's accident had something to do with the way I feel about suicide. You think they're out there doing something safe and then they get hurt anyway. That's another matter of inches and seconds.

"You realize how vulnerable we all are."

A SISTER'S LIFE AND DEATH

Carol V., forty, a former reporter, is now a free-lance writer living in Nevada. Her sister, whom we'll call Meg, was thirty-five when she committed suicide, but she had been making attempts since the age of four. The year before she took her life, she had finally been diagnosed as manic-depressive.

"When we were in our twenties she reminded me that even as a little girl she had thoughts of killing herself. It was frightening to her and she didn't know why.

"She thought the first episode occurred when she was about three, but I remember her being four. I'll never forget that day. I was the one who was three. I remember her hurting herself like that and I wondered why she wasn't crying.

"She said, 'Carol come here.' It was the first time she had ever asked me to help her with anything. She was never too involved with the family — always one step outside. So I went to the bathroom and she climbed on the toilet and got into the cabinet and she handed me down an old Band-Aid box. My dad would put his old razors in there. He changed and got a new one everyday. Some of them spilled out on the floor and my sister said, 'Never mind that,' when I bent down to pick them up. We went back to the bedroom and she asked if I wanted some and I didn't know what to say. I just got back into bed. She very methodically and slowly took one blade after another and cut her right arm and then her left, and she laid back and watched the blood trickle down on the sheet. We were very quiet and she had a vacant look on her face.

"The next thing I remember was mother screaming, 'Oh, my God. What are you doing?' They were superficial cuts and mother cleaned it all up — ripped the sheets off. She was frantic. She didn't call anyone. She took cold towels and wrapped them around Meg's arms. After that, I don't remember what we did.

"The next time she acted out she was eight years old and I was seven. We had moved again. Dad was in the army, and we had moved around with him, and sometimes he'd go overseas for two years and we'd stay home. This time we moved to Wisconsin where my mother's parents lived. We moved in with them. My grandmother was dying of cancer. Mother also took care of her father who was diabetic.

"We were walking to school, a new school, and my mother was holding my sister's hand and all of a sudden she pulled away and ran out in front of an old '54 or '55 Buick. It swerved to keep from hitting her. The man driving the car was shocked and my mother screamed, 'Meg, what are you doing?' and Meg just hung her head as if she had failed again. That look on her face was like a puppy dog who had been shamed. She always had those big, sad brown eyes, and she looked down and didn't say anything. The crossing guard came over and put her arms around Meg.

"Mother didn't seem to understand anything, but it seemed to me that whenever Meg was faced with a new experience, she acted out. That first time, when she was four, she was getting ready to start preschool. When she was eight she was starting a new school, and when she began high school, her problems began to manifest themselves again.

"She was basically a very shy, introverted person. The friends she did make were very close to her, but she always seemed one step removed from what was going on. It was after her third suicide attempt at fourteen, when she took a bottle of aspirin, that Mom took her to a doctor and he recommended a psychologist. So Mom took her. He [the psychologist] never talked to any other members of the family, and every time he talked to my sister, she came out crying.

"Mother also took her to the Christian Science counselor who didn't believe in any of these chemical imbalances. She basically worked with retarded kids and she believed my sister was twelve years old emotionally. She didn't do one thing for Meg, who was in a deep depression by then.

"Meg wasn't bathing or washing her hair and she looked terrible. This counselor would say, 'I don't want you coming back here anymore until you wash your hair and until your appearance is better.'"

Carol says she hated the woman, a view she holds to this day.

"Meg was aware that she was different — that she didn't fit in. She talked a lot about dying. It was like she didn't want to have been born. She didn't want to be in this world with this illness she had. If somebody early on had said, 'Meg, you were born with this chemical imbalance,' and had the illness been explained to her, I think she could have dealt with it."

Meg wasn't truly diagnosed and given medication until about a year before she killed herself. During those intervening years, she dated, eventually married and had two children.

Also during those years, the family disintegrated. "Mom didn't even want to be home. Dad was chronically depressed but hid it by just sitting and watching TV.

"I remember feeling helpless. Here was my sister in desperate need of love — of someone to put their arms around her and say, 'We're going to find out what this is and beat this thing together.' Knowing there was no help for her and probably never would be, it seemed like I was a child myself watching another child being victimized by her illness and her environment.

"Later on we discovered that my father had a brother who was a paranoid schizophrenic. No one ever saw or spoke about his mental illness in those days. It was covered up. Even my dad was ashamed of his own illness. He also had a sister who was agoraphobic and became an alcoholic.

"By the time my sister was eighteen, everybody recognized that she had these real lows and highs. She married when she was twenty-two and I remember she didn't want to marry. He was our next-door neighbor. They got engaged at Christmas and she came up to the bedroom and said, 'I don't love him. It won't work out. But you know how Mom is.'"

Carol recalls that her sister tried to tell her mother how she really felt about getting married, but that her mother panicked. "Mom just wanted her out of her hair. She wanted to wash her hands of it. That was my impression.

"Meg's future husband was studying to be a psychologist and Mom felt that if she married him, it would help her. The marriage was rocky from the start, and grew worse through the years.

"I had to move away. I got to the point I could no longer live with my parents and around my sister. I love my sister, but it was like being on a pier and standing by watching someone drown. I had gotten to the point where I ate my meals in the bedroom."

Eventually Carol moved out of state, but stayed in contact with her family and visited from time to time.

"Meg always talked about how all our lives she wished our parents would show some love. My father gave her a Raggedy Ann doll once — the only thing he ever gave her.

"She kept it on her bed even after she got married. On the morning of her death it was lying there looking down at her. She had taken a bottle of [medication given for manic depression]. She drank the bottle, laid down on the bed, Bible opened to the Twenty-third Psalm, folded her hands in prayer and died."

Her young sons found the body and recounted to Carol that their mother's eyes were open, one staring at the ceiling. The head was twisted and the mouth distorted. "It was a horrible sight for her little boys, but it shows you how the body will fight to live. The body doesn't die easily."

Before Meg's final suicide attempt (there had been others throughout her marriage), Carol had visited her, and recalls Meg saying, "I don't want to die. I don't want to kill myself. But my thoughts get interrupted. It's just that with this illness I have, it makes me think I want to die. I can't think clearly."

Carol is glad that her sister at least understood that it was the illness that made her act irrationally. In a sense, it gave her some feeling of self worth.

"When Meg died, my mother said an interesting thing. She said, 'It took a lot of guts for Meg to kill herself.'

"It bothered me because I wanted to say, 'No, it takes a lot of guts to live.' But in a way, Meg sacrificed herself so her family could get on with living and wouldn't have to be bothered with her. She knew that society couldn't deal with it — that her family couldn't deal with it.

Carol has a lot of bitterness still about how her sister's mental illness was ignored. "The reality is, you're better off dead in this society," she says. "It's better to be born with a deformity that can be seen. It's worse to be born with a mental illness that no one can see. People want to bury it. They don't want to deal with it."

Carol acknowledges that she had to outgrow a lot of anger concerning her childhood and early adult life.

"I don't feel that way now because I have love around me. I had become emotionally cold. I set goals for myself, and it took me a long time to achieve them. That's why I try to be so good to my friends and to do special things for my husband and children."

Carol's mother died at age sixty-six of cancer. Her father moved to Nevada and lives in a retirement home a few miles from her, and Carol has made peace with him, partly by understanding the illness that affected him.

The writing she sells to many magazines is usually concerned with people who have overcome great difficulties in life — their triumphs and tribulations.

Carol's type of writing may inadvertently be a way of

working out the grief of her sister's death, she believes. Many survivors are propelled into not only reaching out to help the community, but in taking up work that helps resolve their own conflicts.

WORKING THROUGH THE GRIEF

Chip Frye, twenty-nine, whose sister committed suicide in 1984 at the age of thirty-two, mans a suicide hotline at the Los Angeles Suicide Prevention Center, which has served as the prototype for other centers throughout the country.

He didn't contact the center until more than a year after his sister's death, and believes it was a critical turning point for him.

He had seen an ad on television asking for volunteers at the center. "I was apprehensive at first because I knew it would bring up a bunch of stuff about my sister's death, and I was very busy at the time, but I took the training, and now I work there from twenty-four to thirty-six hours a week."

Despite his involvement and training, Chip acknowledges that he probably will grieve for his sister the rest of his life.

"I don't think I will ever resolve her suicide. There is just no way to answer certain questions, but I accept that. I've relieved her of the responsibility of having caused this pain for me. For a very long time I cried for the sadness of the loss I felt for her, but one evening just out of nowhere, I finally cried for the joy of just being able to understand what had occurred.

"There will always be the unanswered question of why she killed herself. Why didn't she turn to the family? Why didn't she do anything rather than kill herself? This is our dilemma in being survivors. Unless you are a survivor, there is no way you can even begin to conceive the confusion and inherent tragedy of this self-destruction. You are part of it, regardless of who is responsible," he says.

Chip says he realizes that once the suicide occurs, it is solely the responsibility of the person who takes his or her own life. "When it comes down to responsibility, it is one hundred percent the responsibility of the person who commits suicide. It is a difficult concept to grasp when you have lost a loved one because you feel responsible and so do other family members, but the bottom line is there is no one else responsible except the person who does it — even if they are alcoholics, mentally ill, depressed — no matter how extreme their problem is, it is their choice."

This doesn't prevent him from believing that if his family had mobilized, they might have been able to save her for the time being — "At least to have been able to work on the problem."

His sister was an artist and a virtuoso on the violin. The entire family are artists and musicians and Chip is an actor.

Despite the likenesses in the family, the sisters and brothers were kept in the dark about his sister's problem. "It's not too unusual. Only her husband, my father and a psychiatrist who was seeing her knew that she had been diagnosed as schizophrenic. There was this protection taking place. We were never told what was wrong."

Although Chip realized his sister wasn't functioning too well, he wasn't told of the illness until after her death. "The real tragedy occurred with the purchase of the gun and no effort was made to do anything about it. Neither the psychiatrist nor the husband felt the threat of the gun was serious," he recalls.

Chip is now involved in a training program where volunteers go into junior high and high schools to educate youth about suicide. Through the training he received, he has learned that many teen suicides take place because of the availability of guns in the home. "A youth will decide in a split second that he doesn't want to go on, and because the gun is there in the house, he's able to do something about it. If a means of committing suicide hadn't been so readily available, the youth may have had to wait, and in the meantime get over his self-destructive feelings," says Chip.

Dennis Smith of the Center to Prevent Handgun Violence, and many others, believe that if there were a waiting period for the purchase of guns, the person might have time to think things over and decide not to kill him or herself. As it now stands throughout most of the country, they can walk into a gun shop and purchase a gun to kill themselves immediately.

In 1984 there were 14,487 suicides committed with handguns. In one study of handguns in the home it was found that handguns are three to seven times more likely to be used in an accidental shooting or for suicide than to be used for self defense, according to Jan Kelso of Hand Gun Control Inc. in Washington, D.C.

Psychologist Pamela Cantor, former president of the American Association of Suicidology, says there are more suicides committed with handguns than homicides and accidents.

"My sister used the gun," says Chip. "She went to the mountains by herself and was missing for a couple of days. Hikers found her in her truck."

"It was a real shock because I had no idea of how bad it was for her. This isn't too unusual in families, however. In our society, and particularly in the prior generation, they always try to protect, and often this does more damage than if it were uncovered. The family would have been able to share the problem — 'Let's put our heads together and show them they don't need to die.' Too often there is an isolation there. We need to mobilize as many individuals as possible for intervention."

Like many other survivors, Chip is still angry, but not to the degree he was when it first happened.

"I chose to make a decision that there was no God. I was very vocal about that. There was a priest who came to the house to console us, a grief counselor, and I found that humorous. He wasn't counseling us. He just sat among us. I chose to defy it.

"Now that I have become a Christian, I have come back to God," he says.

Chip says that his new-found faith was partly based on the strength he saw it bring to other survivors, and to potential suicides. "In my own perspective now in dealing with suicidal people, there is no question that religion helps. But you can't employ that at the prevention center. It turns some people off, but if they bring up God, then you can talk to them about it and it helps."

But the most important help, for survivors, and those contemplating suicide, is non-judgmental support. "No matter what the individual has done, and no matter how bad they may be, they need this non-judgmental support," says Chip. Suicidal people also need professional help, of course.

"Ignorance surrounding suicide is absolutely the biggie," Chip says. "We need to educate people about what to do about it. For myself, it was wading through a lot of mud and muck to try and even find a direction with my grief. I didn't know there were survivor's groups and support situations that existed. And it's critical. For example, a friend of mine who had a loved one commit suicide kept perceiving she heard [the deceased's] voice telling her to join him — to commit suicide and be there with him.

"This is a very common occurrence among survivors and when people don't know that, they become fearful and it snowballs and they might be tempted to commit suicide themselves." (Professionals caution that, while having fleeting thoughts of suicide or hearing the voice of the deceased may be common, the repeated experience of having this voice invite one to suicide, as described here, is a serious situation requiring professional help.)

"In the first two weeks, a survivor has sensory overload and can't get in touch with the self. They have no energy and can't even read a book," Chip explains.

Chip says that in survivor's groups people always say they never thought it could happen to them, "but it does. It happens in the nicest of families. That's why it's so frightening."

PARENTS GIVE AND RECEIVE SUPPORT

Ira and Jeanne Jacoves recently celebrated the wedding of a son. It was a joyous occasion, but the absence of another son, Jonathan Jacoves who had killed himself, was felt by all.

"The absence loomed very large," says Jeanne. "The wedding was kind of a culmination. It was different to take family pictures without Jonathan. You just never get over it."

Their son, Jonathan, as described by the father was a "happy-go-lucky, pro tennis player," who killed himself nearly four years ago.

"If there are telltale signs then people who are close can find the problem and get help for them, but it doesn't always help. They commit suicide anyway," says Ira.

Four months prior to his death, the family noticed changes in their son, saw his signs of distress and contacted a psychologist. Jonathan began therapy, and was in and out of hospitals during that four months. Nothing, however, helped. Just after his last release from the hospital he killed himself.

"It's very difficult to accept and live with. You have a lot of self doubts and it takes time to heal. Nothing anybody did helped, except meeting with other survivors. Nothing else was more satisfying than knowing others had gone through and were going through the same thing," says Ira.

Because of the help the couple received through support groups, they established the Jonathan Jacoves Memorial which helps fund support groups for survivors at the University of Judaism in Los Angeles.

Although the Jacoves found the kind of support they were looking for through the groups, Ira is perplexed that more men don't attend them.

"We were the only couple going. Sometimes the husbands won't go, but their wives were there. That's too bad. They need to help each other. If you don't try to understand the situation and the feelings you have, you can't understand your spouse's feelings. You have to understand your partner's problems in order to help.

"I think no matter how hard it is for the father, it's harder for a loving mother. The woman has a different relationship to the child, regardless of what the courts are now saying. The father can be close, but biologically there's a deeper imprint on the woman. I'm not saying it wasn't devastating for me, but I didn't carry that child for nine months," says Ira.

"Whether you're the father or the mother, it helps to talk about it. You just can't keep it in. I had friends who were compassionate and understanding, but for a while, at first, I didn't want to see anyone.

"I ended up changing some of my friends. My outlook changed and I found I didn't need superficial friends. You can tell when someone doesn't want to get involved. Some people would rather close it out. They would say, 'Well, It's over, so get it out of your system.'

"I wanted to hit them. You don't want to hear anything flippant at a time like that. You learn that you don't have that much control over your life, much less someone else's."

Jeanne agrees with her husband. "Society says you're supposed to mourn for just a certain period of time and then get over it — maybe six months, a year — but it's been nearly four years for us, and it's still with us.

"One of the stupidest things people can say is, 'Now you know at least he's at peace.' Jonathan was having problems, that's true. But I think you would rather have the loved one with you even if they are distressed so you could help do something about it.

"I have a friend, and her son had been distressed for a long time and she felt relieved when it was finally over. But not for me. I always think I can fix it.

"One of the reasons we set up a survivors group is that the very term 'prevention' sets in motion that it could have been prevented. If you keep hearing that suicides are all preventable, you start feeling that guilt and blame again," says Jeanne.

"Most of the parents we've dealt with are loving, caring people who had tried to get help for their loved ones once a problem had been recognized. Still, the person committed suicide. You can't do a lot of intervention when the child is twenty-six years old.

"I'm beginning to enjoy life again, but the absence of Jonathan is very present — very real. There was some guilt after the first years when I started enjoying a few things again, but it lessens over time," she says.

Jeanne recently completed private counseling. She's also reentered college working toward a degree in psychology, and she continues to work with support groups.

The couple believes their closeness, and their ability to work through the bereavement together helped, and they are fortunate for this. Too often, couples are torn apart when tragedy strikes a family.

Judith Bernstein, a psychotherapist who specializes in bereavement, and who heads the support groups made possible by the Jacoves' memorial, says that when couples lose a child it often generates a lot of conflict between them. "Each partner has different perceptions of the suicide and they have different responses with one person accepting the suicide and the other denying it."

Statements such as "No, it wasn't a suicide. It was an accident," or "It was your fault because you always gave in and protected him," and "If you hadn't worked as much as you did and had spent more time with the children," cause more grief.

One spouse may also tell the other, "You're blaming yourself too much. It's not your fault. Quit blaming yourself."

"Sometimes the husband will lose patience and tolerance when the wife continues to be engulfed in the grief," says Bernstein.

In reality, if the couple had a shaky marriage to begin with, it may get worse, and if they had a good one, with open lines of communication, they will work with one another and allow each to handle the grief in his or her own way.

TURNING GRIEF INTO ACTION

Following the suicide death of her twenty-one-year-old stepdaughter in 1979, Adina Wrobleski of Minnesota joined the American Association of Suicidology and attended their first national convention. The group was made up of professionals in the field, and Adina was the only survivor there. She says that they were not particularly interested in her perspective. Four years later, however, she began researching suicide and its aftermath in depth, in order to answer some of her own nagging questions. Because her research was so extensive, and because she was coming at the problem from a different angle (as a survivor), she began receiving international attention, and attended the International Symposium on Bereavement in Society, that took place in Jerusalem. At that symposium, she presented one of her research papers on survivors, only to have it selected for publication in the *Israel Journal of Psychiatry.*

"It was the first paper done by an experiential person. There had been some papers done by the professionals on survivors, but they pictured it as pathological, dark, gloomy, and predicted pathological results. Up to that time studies of survivors had been conducted only on clinical patients who had psychiatric disorders or pathological grief reactions, and they had extrapolated from that.

"Up until that time, it was commonly believed that suicide survivors didn't get over their grief, and all needed professional help," she says.

Adina, however, based her studies on ordinary people — ordinary survivors — and found that the dire predictions of the professionals didn't hold up. "Based on my experience and that of others, it just wasn't so," she says.

"What I did was a maverick kind of thing. I didn't have a degree. But what I discovered is that if you have the knowledge you can establish yourself. The professionals accepted me."

When I first began interviewing professionals for this book, her name was frequently mentioned, and one suicidologist said I just had to talk with her.

Her own lonely journey began one night in 1979.

The day her daughter Lynn killed herself, Adina and her husband Hank, "had been feeling particularly happy. It was just one of those happy something days. About six that evening the doorbell rang, and a police officer we knew as a friend was standing there.

"'I have bad news,' he said. 'Lynn is dead. She shot herself.'

"I can remember what must have been shock taking over my body. It was just like a huge iron door had slammed shut. You could feel the impact of it, but you couldn't hear it."

She remembers calling family and friends — "Just calling people over and over. It was sort of a period of being in a red kind of fog.

"The funeral period wasn't any different than what others go through, except people didn't seem to know what to say. I'd say to them, 'I don't care. I'm just glad you came.' I just needed to feel those strokes of love. Some people, virtual strangers, helped. There was a woman next door, a reclusive. I hardly knew her and she brought chicken and cake over. I feel one of the good funeral customs is the bringing of food. I was incapable of preparing anything.

"After the first two weeks, we were by ourselves. That is the telling point — when everyone leaves."

That's when the reflections began. She thought about Lynn's earlier rebellions that had eventually culminated in a close relationship, especially after Lynn married. "That was the end of the pressure cooker stage. After that she kind of blossomed."

Lynn and her husband were getting ready to move into their dream house when she committed suicide.

"Things were going pretty good, and when she did commit suicide, I wasn't aware enough that other things were going on. There were warnings I didn't see. She obviously had depression."

Adina became aware of the darker side to Lynn's life only after her death, and after attending support groups. "It seemed clear that Lynn had depression since she was nine or ten. The big thing nobody knew or recognized was that Lynn had abrupt changes of how she felt about the house that was being built. She began to fear the house. We went to lunch one day and I could see she was in a bad mood. We talked for four hours and I tried to reassure her about it. In the middle of that long conversation she laughed and said she'd had a gun to her head twice. I was so frightened I didn't know what to say or do.

"That just shows you how strong denial is. My experience now is that when suicide survivors are faced with this, the only recourse is denial. I felt helpless. I know now that I should have taken her to the hospital. So I am telling people to pay attention to these signs."

"Right in this great big restaurant she said, 'Thanks for caring about me.' I now think she was saying goodbye. But at the time I was puzzled and disturbed and told Hank about it when I got home."

Adina recalls that Lynn had fears about going to war with Russia, and the family tried to comfort her. "She'd hear something on the radio and would worry that the world was coming to an end.

"Anyway, the day after our conversation in the restaurant, she called three times and seemed confused. She'd say, 'Tell me again what it was you said yesterday.'

"Her last day she got up and got dressed. She didn't go to work. There are people who say you never know why people kill themselves. I know Lynn died because of depression, but the 'why' that haunts me is that moment she decided, 'Now is the time.'"

Adina's voice becomes a whisper and the words are spoken with trembling lips while she talks about how people do get over the suicide, but at the same time, the tragedy stays with them.

"One of the things I'm against is the belief that suicide death is something you'll never get over, or that it will take years. The sense in which that is true is that it is such an awful thing. As you can see, I can go back there and relive the entire thing. However, I have this personal concept that inside a person is a little black pool of unhappiness where all the bad things that happen are put. Then I use the metaphor of a river, and coming back to walk on the ice on the river. Periodically we fall down into the black pool, but then we go on. As you get on through time you fall less far, and you don't fall as often.

"There is life after suicide. But we not only go through the grieving process that others do; we also have these extra things. You think if you had been kinder, better, loved more, listened more carefully, she wouldn't have died. This is the assumption you see in language. In no other death do people say, 'Oh, that poor family. They must feel terribly guilty.' We don't make this assumption with other deaths."

But Adina is optimistic. "I think the stigma is lessening. We can have control over it. There are things we can do to prevent suicide. We can start treating the mental illnesses that can result in suicide medically and psychologically. We can get rid of our old beliefs."

3

RELIGIOUS PERSPECTIVES

G ILBERT E. BRODIE of King's College in Canada says in a paper published in *Death Studies* that suicide can seriously undermine the self-esteem of the survivors. "The experience of guilt and shame so often found among the survivors of a suicide is not unrelated to the same feelings found in the battered or abused child or wife. All have been assaulted by loved ones. Time and again we are told by survivors that the guilt goes beyond what we are likely to feel after any other kind of death. What they are experiencing is not just the normal loss but also the inescapable intimidation of rejection."

This intimidation is compounded when the survivors feel rejected by the church. This is infrequent today, however. Most religious communities, while not condoning suicide, empathize with the deceased and offer love and compassion to the survivors.

Many survivors report that their church or synagogue is one of the greatest sources of comfort in dealing with the tragedy that has entered their lives.

A good portion of the clergy of all faiths recognize that a suicidal person is not rational, and therefore, not accountable for his or her actions.

On the other hand, some religious leaders acknowledge that within the church, no serious discussion of suicide takes place — that the clergy skirts the hard issues of just what the act implies for the person who commits suicide.

When the mother of Monette L. committed suicide and preparations were being made for her funeral, Monette candidly asked the officiating minister if he had any problems with the thought of conducting the services for her mother. She said that if he did have reservations, they would get someone else.

"I was ready to fight," she recalls, "But it wasn't necessary."

Speaking forthrightly about this saved the entire family much grief. They were assured that the services for their mother would be carried out in a dignified and loving manner.

Christian tradition today holds a variety of views on suicide. Catholics once considered it a mortal sin, but today they don't believe suicides are responsible for their act.

Father Peter Covas of Holy Rosary Church in San Bernardino, California said the change occurred about twenty-five years ago. Prior to that it was considered a 'public scandal' and burial within the church was forbidden.

"The thinking now is that when the person reaches the stage where they are really contemplating suicide, they're not in control of their real faculties. So before God there is no offense," he says.

"That is one place where the church has more or less changed its attitude," says Sister Jane Frances Power, direc-

tor of the Health and Hospital Department for the Archdio-
cese of Los Angeles. "It used to think it was a deliberate
thing, and was therefore sinful. But it has been many years
since that attitude was held by the church. The proof of that
is that they say a memorial mass for the individual. When I
was young they didn't say that mass.

"They used to think the person was totally in their
right mind when they did it, but we know today that they do
it under different circumstances and aren't competent. As
far as condemning them and saying they are going to Hell,
we don't do that. The individual state of mind is what deter-
mines that and that is between the person and God.

"I would counsel anyone the same as with any other
bereavement. Of course, if they feel that the loved one did
something wrong, that is a terrible burden to bear. I would
emphasize that the person was under stress and strain and
that his motives are left to God," adds Sister Jane Frances.

Some protestant groups believe suicide is a sin, but
not an unforgivable one, and still other protestant bodies
believe that suicide has nothing to do with the person's
relationship with God.

"The average person who commits suicide has no
desire to die. They are reaching out and struggling. The line
is so fine. Many don't intend to commit suicide. It's just one
of those things we have to deal with in life. I certainly give
assurance that we don't hold any type of belief in sin when
people commit suicide. Basically, it's one of the mysteries of
life," says Covell Hart of the First Presbyterian Church in
Elsinore, California.

Covell holds a doctorate of divinity, and his wife,
Phyllis, who co-pastors with him, has a doctorate in psychology and a master of divinity.

"I think suicide is one of the serious problems of the
church that we're going to have to deal and cope with. One
of the big reasons the churches are losing a lot of people is

that they have brushed aside things like suicide and divorce and abortion, even when the reality of it all hits home. They just don't know how to handle these things. They can't preach something they've always preached the opposite about, so it makes it very hard," says Covell.

"If the survivor believed their loved one was going to Hell, how could they get through the suicide?" he asks. "People don't really believe this, and neither do church leaders. They just brush it aside.

"There are no easy answers, especially with the new information on depression and suicide. Once the brain chemicals have been altered these people aren't rational — aren't responsible for their actions," says Phyllis.

"If we were counseling a family of a suicide and if they asked if the person was going to Hell, or if it was a sin, I'd say, 'Absolutely not,'" adds Covell. "They just went through some real confusing difficult times."

Covell knows from whence he speaks. He attempted suicide more than twenty years ago after his first wife asked for a divorce.

He went out to the garage, closed the door, turned on the car's motor and waited to die. "It was about 2:00 A.M. and this widow lady who lived down the street was driving home and her car died. She got out to see if she could get help at our house because the lights were on. She heard the engine running, looked through the garage door, saw me slumped over the wheel and went and got someone to help break down the door."

Covell shares his experience with those he counsels, and members of his church are well aware of his attempt.

"I was unconscious for a couple of days. I tell people now that I didn't really want to die. I was crying out for help."

An unusual twist to this story is that right after he got out of the hospital he received a phone call from a friend in New York that he hadn't heard from in twenty years. The friend said that she woke up in the middle of the night and was obsessed with thoughts of him. She woke up her husband and he joined her in prayer for Covell without even knowing what had happened.

The woman contacted Covell a few days later after obtaining his phone number from an alumni association.

"It's such a fine line. If that hadn't happened in the car twenty years ago, I wouldn't have met Phyllis and had all this happiness with the church. These later years since the attempt have been the happiest in my life. If I had been successful with the suicide I wouldn't have had this chance," he reflects.

Because of his experiences, Covell believes it makes him more understanding when dealing with any type of trauma confronting a family.

At the time of his suicide attempt and subsequent divorce, the church body he was affiliated with offered little support and comfort. He changed his affiliation and now counsels not only parishioners and other members of the community, but is often called upon to advise other ministers of various denominations who are faced with adversity in their own lives and who need understanding support.

Phyllis and Covell acknowledge that many religious leaders just don't understand suicide and have a difficult time ministering to survivors.

Phyllis, too, early on learned about suicide the hard way, and from those experiences developed a more enlightened attitude about it. One event involved a young couple who were friends of hers. "The husband was a super guy and he died suddenly of a freak illness. Several months later the wife was extremely depressed and seeing a psychiatrist. Nevertheless, she took her youngest child into the garage and told him they were going to go see his daddy. She spared her two older children. The younger child died in her arms of carbon monoxide poisoning.

"We should have paid more attention to her depression. We even said we 'should have done this...should have done that.' It was a tremendous devastation."

Another event that caused Phyllis to take a second look at suicide occurred early in her career when she was working at a psychiatric facility. One of the patients, whose husband of many years suddenly walked out of their marriage, was continually asking about suicide. "She seemed too crazy to commit suicide and we disregarded her comments such as, 'If I put a rope around my neck will I die?' Well, the woman did commit suicide. We learned a lot of lessons from her. We know now to pay attention. Those who are left have to deal with the guilt."

Although many in the mental health community say that the leading cause of suicide is severe depression, schizophrenia and manic-depression, others don't agree. Covell and Phyllis are among those who believe most suicidal behavior is caused by depression or mental illness.

"The problem is, how do you know if someone is depressed? This is especially difficult when dealing with teenagers. They don't talk to their parents much anyway. Their friends may know, and they may worry, but they don't tell the parents," says Phyllis.

When a teen commits suicide, everyone is devastated.

"Psychologically, for the survivors, there are initial emotions of anger which are very rarely expressed. There is the usual sadness and grief, and that is expressed, but not the anger, especially if it is a grieving parent. Yet, they have the anger, but it doesn't come out," Phyllis says.

The entire area of grief over a suicide death is muddied. "There is a kind of popular view that grief is only supposed to take a certain time, but this is not realistic. It is a recurring emotion. Grief is not a constant emotion, and the less you have dealt with it intensely it will stay relatively untouched and pop out every once in a while," says Phyllis.

Jewish tradition sets guidelines for mourning, and Rabbi Marvin Goodman believes they help, especially in the case of suicide because they offer assistance at a time when the sur-vivors have lost any conception of what's expected of them.

There is the initial seven days of mourning where the family members don't leave the house. People come to them bringing food and condolences. This is a period of intense mourning. No one expects the family to do anything, and the family is comforted because nothing is expected of them. Mirrors in the house are covered so that the person is free to deal only with his or her inward feelings.

For the next thirty days the grieving is not so intense, but the family is free to not do anything. At the end of about a year, a ceremony to dedicate the tombstone — an unveiling — takes place. This signifies the end to the intense mourning period. "It isn't that the person will ever get over the grief of the death — you never wholly get over that," says Goodman.

Jewish ritual gave him direction when a youth he had known and worked with committed suicide. Goodman was out of the country for four months and was unable to take part in the funeral. But he conducted the tombstone dedication and said, "It gave me the opportunity to express my words and feelings. I hadn't been there to cry with the family when it happened."

Goodman felt particularly grieved because the youth, who had obviously been having problems for some time, never confided in anyone. "I thought I knew this kid. I worked with him for several years, and I saw this strong, popular, seemingly articulate kid, and found out he had all these problems he never told anybody about. It just tore him up inside, and he didn't confide in anyone. A suicide can't be blamed for what they have done. The good in that person's life certainly outweighs the tragedy," says Goodman.

In Jewish tradition there have always been acceptable reasons for suicide, some of which are illustrated in the Bible, such as the attack at Masada where Jews took their own lives rather than surrender to the enemy.

During the Christian Crusades, crusaders on their way to the Holy Land would attack Jewish communities and try to force baptism. Whole communities committed suicide rather than be baptized. "And during the Holocaust, we definitely know there were more suicides, especially those engaged in the resistance and couriers in the ghetto. They committed suicide rather than be caught and tortured," says Rabbi Ben Zion Bergman at the University of Judaism in Los Angeles.

Zdzislaw Ryn, M.D. of Poland, who researched war records, says that thousands of people killed themselves when conditions were at their worst between 1940 and 1942.

"In a situation when death seemed to be a question only of time, many prisoners shortened the period of time 'to become free' earlier," he writes. "It is certain that suicidal death was a mass phenomenon in camp conditions, and that uncounted masses of prisoners were its victims."

In the past, Jewish culture has had one of the lowest suicide rates, but it is nearly equal that of Christianity today. Because of the growing problem of suicide, national Jewish task forces have been instituted to deal with the problem.

"In general we're catching up with the general community in lots of ways. We used to also have a very low divorce rate. The changes are the price of our integration into general society. As we become acculturized to the specific demands and influences of the general culture, our traditions become less potent," says Rabbi Bergman.

Bergman says that the breakdown of the family contributes to the increase in suicide "because the force of the tradition has been weakened."

Like the Christian tradition, Judaism has, through the

ages, softened its harsh stand against suicide. "Every sin is forgivable in Judaism," says Bergman, but traditionally a suicide was treated as absolutely the worst of malefactors. The suicide wasn't buried within the burial ground and the early commentators forbade the eulogizing of the suicide. The family wasn't to observe the rites of mourning.

By the eighteenth century, there was still no eulogy allowed, but for the family's sake they were allowed to observe the rite of the seven days of mourning.

In a later attempt to ameliorate the harshness of the laws Jewish authorities said that while it was true that the person had done something to take his own life, it was unknown whether or not he repented in the instant before he took his life and it was also possible that he wasn't in his right mind — distraught with the pain and not really responsible, according to Bergman.

"For the parents, it's easy for them to feel guilt, and I try to point out that there are many influences and forces at work today that are beyond parental influences. The thrust of today's Judaism is to give comfort to the family," adds Bergman.

H. Newton Malony, Ph.D., professor of psychology and theology associated with Fuller Theological Seminary in Pasadena, California, agrees that the main responsibility of the church is to give comfort to the bereaved.

Malony has also been intimately touched by suicide, and holds another view on how a Christian deals with its aftermath. He believes suicide is a sin, but not an unforgivable one.

Those who have been raised with the ideology that suicide is a "deadly sin" should "put their reliance on a merciful God," says Malony. "God is simply more in the forgiving business than the judging business."

"Suicide is born out of great travail. Some have said it is an aggressive, hostile act, but I think it is a troubled soul who wants to get out from under the stress they're under. God is merciful there, although He doesn't take the sadness or mystery away, or the perplexity or confusion as to why someone would commit suicide.

"The Christian faith functions as comfort and it is no different in the ways we are confronted with other tragedies of life — the other perplexities and enigmas of life which don't make a lot of sense."

"You simply rest back on the sovereignty and mercy of God."

Malony believes that the most important question facing survivors isn't their perplexity as to why the person committed suicide, but the overall confusion and ambivalence survivors feel.

"The person simply has to let go, and that's tough," acknowledges Malony.

"What is going to happen to them? They're kept in turmoil because there are no real answers. I've heard survivors say they've felt the presence or the spirit of the suicide victim hovering around, and if it is a hostile presence, it is a frightening thing."

As well as counseling survivors, Malony has had firsthand experience in dealing with suicide. First, when he was in seminary school more than thirty years ago when a close friend jumped out of a church tower.

"It led me to contemplate my own suicide, and I think that's part of the ripple effect — why sometimes you have one suicide following another. It led me to believe that if he doubted his faith, maybe I wasn't so sure of mine either. I was going through my own intellectual crisis at the time — 'Do I believe in God?' — and I think that's pretty typical. You start asking yourself, 'Does life have meaning?'"

His friend's suicide shook up that belief because, "Part of your sense that life has meaning is that those about you also affirm its meaning. If that is shaken by someone close to you saying 'life doesn't have meaning, and I'm going to take myself out of it,' your buttress is shaken. That is the ripple effect. There is this implicit, unconscious dependence on this person confirming your existence.

"That's why there is so much anger associated with suicide, and I believe the anger is healthy. My understanding is that where that can occur early, as well as the sadness, the grieving is lessened.

"Anger is energy turned outward as opposed to depression which is anger turned inward. So showing anger is much more healthy than turning inward and blaming the self.

"We could easily blame ourselves — 'I could have done such and such' — but the thing is, the person is going to do it if they are going to do it. They will find a way."

I interviewed Malony only three months after another close friend of his had committed suicide. Malony had officiated at the man's wedding years ago, and also when he had renewed his wedding vows three days before the suicide.

"All things seemed to be going uphill for him," says Malony.

"You do have to say that the Christian faith functions in several ways. One is comfort. Another is challenge, and another is the call to right living. But in this case, the Christian faith functions as comfort and it is no different in the ways we are comforted during other tragedies of life."

In the book *After Suicide,* John H. Hewett, a Baptist pastor, says that the survivors need to rid themselves of the superstition that all suicides go to Hell. "This often results from a rigid logic which teaches that forgiveness occurs only after repentance. I believe the wealth of the Biblical evidence shows that God's grace and mercy are unmerited, given freely. We don't earn his love, we receive it."

Other superstitions that have found their way into popular belief stem from Eastern traditions.

A friend of mine whose husband deserted her when she was forty-five went into a deep depression for several years. Many of us feared she might take her own life. One time I bluntly asked her if she was contemplating suicide and she answered, "I was seriously considering it a few months ago, but an acquaintance of mine told me that if I committed suicide I'd have to come back in the next life and live this one all over until I came to terms with it. The idea of having to live this life over again is worse than going on with it now."

This belief seems to stem from an erroneous conception of Buddhism.

Buddhism, which had its origins in central and eastern Asia in the sixth century B.C., teaches that right thinking and self-denial enables the soul to reach Nirvana, a divine state of release from misdirected desire. It has a growing constituency in the United States.

The Venerable Dr. Havanpola Ratanasara, president of the Buddhist Sangha Council of Southern California, says, "Looking at the life in Buddhism is quite different than the general perception in America. We think life, as a whole, is a continuous flux. Life itself doesn't end with the death, so as long as there is a desire to the attachment to life, then life will continue.

"If the person has done something really morally good, he is sure to be born again in a good state. That is one thing. The other thing is, Buddhists are not equipped to feel bad about death. We are experiencing it at all times. Life has three characteristics. One, arising; two, existing; and three, dying — one after the other. We don't see all this through our eyes, that everything is changing at all times, so when things do change, we become sad. But one shouldn't be sad. There is no reason to grieve yourself.

"When a person comes into the world, they are alone. They don't give any notice that they will be here on such and such day, and what they are to be named. It is purely individualistic, and the kind of relationships one deals with in life aren't the permanent things. Relationships are built after birth. Once the person dies these relationships are over.

"A person shouldn't get strong attachments to life or to anything. Follow the middle path and don't get unduly attached to anything. Learn to understand the nature of change."

Ratanasara believes this type of thinking, although it doesn't negate love of someone else, lessens the suffering due to another's loss.

"Each individual has the responsibility to maintain his or her own life, and one is not given the authority to kill others or themselves. But if they do commit suicide, if they can't face the problems of life, it is their responsibility and not that of the survivors.

"With the Buddhist teaching, life is a continual process. In the course of one's life, certain things in the previous life follow the person, due to their karmic results."

The karmic influence may lead them to suicide, but this doesn't necessarily mean they will come back in another life to finish the one they didn't complete, as is believed by some. "We don't know what karmic influences they will have in their next life," he says.

"The suicide is not a free man, so they are to be pitied," says Ratanasara. "Sure we feel sorry for the person, but we understand the realities of it. It is human nature to feel sorry, but we don't continue to do it."

Offerings, or the practice of *dana,* whereby food is brought to the temple where the monks live, and a ceremony that is performed are the two rituals practiced in the name of the departed. But the practitioners know the deceased will be back in another life, so they don't worry about him, according to Ratanasara.

Many people raised in Western culture may find difficulty in accepting Ratanasara's views, because they seem harsh to us. Few survivors, however, would argue with the idea that they want to get on with life. That's why it's important to listen to the survivors, because they are the ones who hold the key to greater understanding.

It is they who are forcing society's religions to come to grips with suicide — to bring it out into the open for a long, overdue airing.

4
HISTORICAL PERSPECTIVES

Suicide has been with us since the beginning of time. It affects all races and creeds, people of all socioeconomic background; and it's been the subject of debate throughout recorded history.

Louis I. Dublin, writing in *Suicide*, states, "In classical literature as in the sacred writing of the Brahmins and Buddhists there is considerable contradiction regarding the morality of suicide. Most authorities, however, seem agreed that suicide was not considered a sin in the Greek or Roman State; that it was mentioned with a certain degree of admiration in ancient legends and in Homer; that it was opposed by Pythagoras and other early philosophers; that the later schools of Greek and Roman philosophy took a more lenient attitude; and that the Cynics, the Cyrenaics, the Stoics and the Epicureans rather actively encouraged it. All these groups tended to regard life as of little importance, although their emphases on its value were quite different."

Dublin says there are only four instances of individual suicide in the Old Testament: Samson, Saul, Abimelech (wounded by a stone cast by a woman in the siege of the tower of Thebez), and Ahithophel (whose counsel was rejected by Absalom). All of these men were given ritual burial.

William Graham Sumner, author of *Folkways,* points out there was a general weariness of life in the early Christian era that accounted for the readiness to commit suicide and that caused indifference to martyrdom.

"Men fled from the world; pessimism took possession of the people; there was the longing for a better life; the struggle for redemption from this world and from the sins of the flesh and the longing to come before the face of the highest God, there to live forever. It followed naturally that the list of illustrious Greeks and Romans who committed suicide was a long one. Though suicide continued on a large scale during the first and second centuries and Romans of wealth and rank embraced it with astonishing frequency, the attitude of the Christian Church from the time of St. Augustine (the fifth century) diametrically reversed this situation, and during the time when the Catholic Church held sway in Europe, suicide was practically unknown," wrote Sumner.

Dublin writes that, "The early Christians apparently accepted the prevailing attitudes of their time on suicide, particularly when persecution made life unbearable for them. The Apostles did not denounce suicide; the New Testament touched on the question only indirectly, and for several centuries the leaders of the Church did not condemn the practice, which apparently was rather common."

St. Pelagia and St. Jerome approved of some suicides. St. Augustine was the first to denounce suicide as a crime. By the time of Thomas Aquinas (the thirteenth century), suicide was considered not only a sin, but a crime as well.

Aquinas carried it further and said a suicide was worse

than a murderer because a self-murderer kills both the body and the soul, but a murderer only kills the body, according to Edward Westermarck writing in *Sociological Review*.

This attitude prevailed throughout the Middle Ages and persisted until about the nineteenth century in England, and in some communities, persisted into the twentieth century.

During the Middle Ages the corpse was often mutilated, and up until the nineteenth and into the twentieth centuries suicides were denied Christian burial, the body was dragged through the streets or hung on the public gallows; left out in the open to be devoured by birds of prey.

Frequently the surviving family members had to move from the community and establish new lives — if that were at all possible. It is no wonder that even today, given this historical background, suicide is often "hidden in the closet."

The old attitudes may have been intended to deter suicide, but there were still instances of mass suicides during the Crusades; sporadic mass outbreaks of suicide among Christians due to religious hysteria, persecution and catastrophe; and great numbers of suicide during pestilence, such as the bubonic plague, sometimes called "Black Death," that killed more than twenty-five million people in fourteenth century Europe.

As other church bodies, such as the Anglican church, became more prominent, some developed more humane attitudes toward suicide.

Since the turn of the century, it has been psychiatrists, psychologists, sociologists, philosophers and the newer branch of suicidology and its researchers who have promoted a more humane attitude about suicide, although all aren't in agreement with one another.

The French sociologist Emile Durkheim wrote in 1897 that suicide must be looked at in its social context rather than isolated individual motives. He calls suicide a normal and not an abnormal reaction to a society that isn't fulfilling the needs of all its members.

Today's professionals involved in the study of suicidal behavior believe that we need to take a new look at society's perception of suicide.

"Suicide is an unexpected form of death. Because of this, there is a judgment made, not only of the deceased but of the survivors. So we need to reexamine this. One thing is that the survivor feels rejected, and they take on more responsibility for the death than is realistic. Part of that grows from the fact that people believe the suicide should have been prevented," says Terrence Barrett, a counseling psychologist at Moorhead State University, Minnesota.

"When it's felt that the suicide should have been prevented, that places the burden on somebody. In retrospect they say, 'How could that have happened?' It's a fact of life that not all suicides can be prevented. And it's hard to present that fact without sounding like you're condoning suicide, and I'm not," adds Barrett.

About half the survivors he counsels take offense at the thought that the suicide might not have been preventable. It offers relief to the other half. "Most of the ones who take offense are burdened by the responsibility," he says.

"Some people aren't able to condone a death that they don't find acceptable, and that's the perception of the general population — that it's not acceptable. Still, it's going to happen, and we don't understand the dynamics of suicide enough to prevent all of it."

Some believe that the only way to prevent suicide is to improve the quality of life, but Barrett points out that "quality of life" is a subjective thing. "You look at someone who is well employed and seems in good stable condition with seemingly happy relationships, and they kill themselves. Then you have to look at the people living on the streets and some of them are still hanging in there."

Obviously, the condition of a society as a whole plays a part in suicide, however.

The suicide rate in the United States increased to about 17 per 100,000 during the Great Depression of the 1920s and '30s, while the normal rate varies between 10-14 per 100,000.

"To me, suicide is still a great mystery," says Barrett. Attempts to unlock the mystery began in the late 1950s and early '60s. Ironically, it began in part with the introduction of psychotropic medications designed to control psychotic symptoms.

"What was noticed at that time was an increase in the rate of suicide among those who were using the drugs. Within the Veterans Administration hospitals it became a matter of great concern," says Dr. Normal L. Farberow, who with Dr. Edwin S. Shneidman, was asked by the government to investigate the problem.

"We found that it wasn't the result of the administration of these medications that made them go out and commit suicide, but medication inhibited their personal contact and involvement with the staff members at the hospital where they had been in therapy," Farberow says.

Farberow, who is presently co-director of the Los Angeles Suicide Prevention Center, says that this realization prompted the government to underwrite further research.

The Veterans Administration established a research center headed by Shneidman and Farberow. This occurred at a time when the country's entire mental health community had begun to expand, taking into its grasp an endeavor to uncover some of the mysteries surrounding suicide.

Some European nations, primarily England, Vienna and Austria had already begun extensive research on suicide prevention.

The research on both continents awakened the interest of the general public. "One of our earliest interests was to do something to dispel the many taboos that surrounded suicide. We were concerned with attacking particular taboos that prevented people from getting help. For a long time it was considered to be a cowardly, weak, unmanly or crazy act," explains Farberow.

These taboos caused those who were suicidal to keep it hidden and to suffer the consequences.

"We were concerned that they should feel open enough about it that they would be able to announce that they felt suicidal and ask for help, and also that the people they would announce it to would not try to deny it and turn away from those who were crying out for help," Farberow says.

Prior to conducting research for the Veteran's Administration, Farberow and Shneidman, with a grant from the National Institute of Mental Health, had established the first suicide prevention center in Los Angeles. It was geared not only to prevention, but to research, training and education, and served as a prototype for others that were later established throughout the country. Here, some of the first support groups for survivors of suicide were established.

"Suicide will always be with us. Probably some suicides can't be prevented, and I don't like to say that. But we'd like to have it at a minimal level," says Farberow.

Farberow adds that the moods of society have a lot to do with the suicide rate. "For the past few decades it has been between 12 and 13 per 100,000 population. It was at its lowest ever in 1956 when it went way down to 9 per 100,000.

"That was a period of great affluence. The whole economy was booming. We had just come out of the Korean War. There was a tremendous feeling of optimism," he says.

Farberow sees suicide prevention as an ongoing battle. Society is starting to dissolve some of the stigma attached to suicide, research continues to uncover the mysteries surrounding it, and suicide prevention has been added to our lexicon.

But other social issues will also have to be addressed. It isn't only affluence, and "good times" that will lower suicide rates. Much depends on the self-worth of individuals and whether or not they are accepted by society.

For example, one high-risk group for suicide appears to be Vietnam veterans. Studies have shown that Vietnam-era veterans are up to twice as likely to commit suicide as non-vets, according to Dr. Norman Hearst of the University of California, San Francisco. Whether this has to do with war-related psychological trauma or the individual's experience re-integrating into society, or both is not known.

Another high-risk group appears to be homosexuals, according to some suicidologists. Although there are no statistics on the number of homosexuals who commit suicide, many professionals agree that it probably is higher than the norm. "It isn't because they are homosexual, but because they sometimes lack the support and understanding that others can count on," says Farberow.

Now, too, there is the added influence of AIDS, in both the homosexual community and the community at large.

It's hardly a secret that many AIDS patients choose to end their own lives, according to Martin Finn, M.D., medical director of the AIDS Program Office for the Los Angeles County Department of Health Services.

Yet many AIDS patients come through fighting for life as never before. "They get additional strength to fight AIDS and it spills over into other areas of their lives. They become real soldiers. They say they want to become examples to others. They have hope and want to give hope to others," Finn emphasizes.

Sister Jane Frances acknowledges that suicide among AIDS patients is prominent. But she says she hopes to eliminate some of the pain by establishing caring places for them to die.

To this end, she has helped develop six residences in cooperation with Catholic hospitals where AIDS patients who have no one to care for them can go.

"That's the purpose of our residences. We've already seen that those who are dying are saying they couldn't have lasted if they hadn't had such a peaceful place to die — one of compassion, love and understanding," says Frances.

It is certainly not unusual for someone diagnosed with a life-threatening illness to consider suicide or, in the later stages of the illness when a great deal of pain is present, to desire euthanasia. Here again, all areas of society are fragmented. One major church study called the issue of euthanasia a "primary spiritual and moral crucible of this age."

Although assisting a person to die by administration of drugs is illegal, the courts are softening their stance and allowing the refusal of treatment by extraordinary measures.

"If we control the birth process, we can control the death process," says Robert Gable, professor of psychology at Claremont Graduate School.

Gable works with hospice patients, and believes that not only does society have to begin addressing the misconceptions about suicide in order to prevent more of them, but in order to enhance the lives of everyone involved.

He emphasizes that suicide is only one of the ethical questions that society must come to grips with, and that other issues, including euthanasia, birth control, abortion, and drug use and abuse, are all entwined in unresolved mystery and conflict.

Using drugs as an example, Gable says both drug use and abuse are a result of our "increasing knowledge about chemicals that can alter our states. We can control these states through chemicals that we weren't familiar with before."

Some drugs are helpful, as in the case of treating depressed or disturbed people. "But we don't yet have a rational policy on how we are going to use psychoactive materials. We have a policy of 'Just say no to drugs.'" So we have conflicting messages.

"Our ethics haven't kept up with our technology. We are a high information society where anyone can know anything. This means we are going to gradually increase and demand control of the quality of our consciousness.

"Society has to take a new look at these issues. Religious bodies tend to be stabilizing forces in a culture. So just as the Catholic Church is wrestling with what to do about birth control, we're wrestling with what to do about death control. There is a place in culture for a stabilizing church, but it is technology that will drag the church, kicking and screaming into the twenty-first century."

"I'm not blaming the church. Technology is just way ahead of our philosophies. We only invent philosophies after technology.

"So we're left with unanswered ethical questions about suicide, and its companion, euthanasia. Yes, technically, euthanasia is illegal. As it is now, it's being done all over the country, even though it isn't popularly accepted. People don't realize the extent it is being done. Almost everyone says that when they are dying they want the choice. But no one is making these decisions and saying, 'Okay,'" says Gable.

"Many hospice patients are older patients dying of cancer. They're given morphine, which is opium. The sick rooms in this country are the modern opium dens, only they are dismal. You wouldn't choose that setting if you had a choice. What the mind sees is what we are prepared to see. If we had the choice, we would choose a place of beauty, we would die in a place with flowers, music and friends. Yet, we let people die in darkened places — isolated and with no friends around because we're afraid to deal with death," Gable says.

This fear of death is just one part of the conflicting emotions society has toward suicide. Like AIDS, death, dying and euthanasia, it is clear that suicide is not a single issue problem. It is related to a plethora of conditions affecting the lives of our multi-cultural, diversified society. It calls out for new understandings in many areas of life, and death.

5

SUICIDE MYTHS

A RECENT SEARCH of the English-language medical literature on suicide yielded more than one thousand papers published since 1982. Additionally, there is vast literature in the religious, philosophical, ethical and legal press, and numerous books and conferences are being devoted to the topic.

This heightened interest in research is shedding new light on what was once a taboo subject, causing many of the myths surrounding suicide to tumble down. Some of the findings are controversial and all aren't in agreement with one another. But a keener knowledge of suicide in general is one way to advance its prevention.

Caution, however, is needed. "We always believe we can make everything right. We're only at the very beginning of what suicide is — the beginning of education on it. There are many different theories on what causes suicide. As we get more research and find out more about it, the existing theories will be reduced. We have hundreds of theories, and they're a dime a dozen. Correct theories are very rare," says David P. Phillips, sociology professor at the University of California, San Diego.

Understanding suicide is presently at about the same stage Sudden Infant Death Syndrome (SIDS) was thirty years ago — full of myths, accusations, misunderstanding, guilt and trauma, especially for the survivors. Thus, much new research is geared to helping the survivors, as well as potential suicides.

Suicide is simply not part of our everyday consciousness, and because of this, we've developed a great mythology to explain its existence, causes, outcome and aftermath.

Dr. R.D.T. Farmer, professor at Charing Cross and Westminster Medical School in London, says, "There are many possible explanations for the fascination that we have with suicide, and for the romanticism that surrounds its portrayal in fine art, literature, and theater. Perhaps the most likely is that self-destruction is perceived as being so unnatural as to excite emotions such as fear, revulsion, and recrimination."

I was speaking to a college writing class and mentioned that the latest book I was working on was for the survivors of suicide. Once the topic was mentioned, electricity seemed to fill the room and the students never let me finish the writing presentation. They simply couldn't break away from the questions they had on suicide. As it turned out, of the twenty-seven students there, all but two of them had recently been touched by suicide, either of friends or acquaintances, or close family members.

One woman asked for the phone number of any support groups in the community. Her sister-in-law had committed suicide over the weekend. She acknowledged that her first emotion was one of anger.

None in the room had ever heard that some researchers believe that a great percentage of young people's suicide might be caused by undiagnosed manic-depression, schizophrenia or severe depression.

Most believed that one person could cause another to commit suicide, and one man became quite angry and said, "Of course a person can tip another over the edge."

"Not unless that person is ready to be tipped," I countered.

The instructor of the class related a story about a friend whose son had committed suicide and how the mother was able to let out her grief but the father had kept it inside for six years and is still suffering. Another man in the class countered with, "The fact that the father is still grieving shows there was something wrong with the family."

The instructor, a friend of mine, shot back with, "That's the type of prejudice we're trying to overcome."

My experience with the class was overwhelming and I was surprised by the hostility of some of the students regarding new research and thinking about suicide.

Many still seemed to have a need to place blame. One man said vehemently, "It just has to be someone's fault."

When the class finally broke up (far past the allotted time), one woman showed me a list of names she had written down during the discussion. "Here are the names of six people I've known who have committed suicide in the past few years," she said.

Another class member, Mary Ortega, later sent me a story she had written about her grandmother's death. I'm sharing it here because it illustrates what may, perhaps, be the biggest myth of all — that somehow, some way, someone other than the suicide victim is responsible for the death.

"My grandmother had been ill of some seemingly undiagnosed disease when I was about eight years old. She had been bedridden but lucid for a period of at least a year.

"A week before her death she got out of bed and tried to do housework. The doctor said she was not physically able to even stand on her feet. She was operating on mental power alone. She insisted that she was a burden to my grandfather and he would be better off if she were dead.

"On the morning of her death, Granddaddy, who slept in the same room, awoke about dawn. Seeing she was not in her bed, he became alarmed and started looking for her. All the doors and windows were either locked or latched from the inside. He looked in the closets, under the beds, even in the cedar chest and kitchen cupboards. He couldn't find her.

"Desperate, he called his son-in-law, Ialy, who lived nearby. Ialy disregarded all the places already searched and went directly to the screened in back porch which housed two wells. One was quite large and contained an electric pump for the house plumbing. The top of this well was bolted down. A small portion of the porch had been walled up to make a room that encompassed the second well. This well was about three-and-a-half feet high with an opening of only one square foot, for emergency use in case the electricity went out.

"A chair stood by the well and the top was laying on the floor. Grandmother was in this well. After her removal, the doctor concluded she had been submerged for several hours.

"My mother got the message by telephone. She was hysterical and could not understand why they were not using artificial respiration to revive her. Even after she was told the neck had been broken in the fall, she refused to believe that Granny was dead. Viewing the body made no impression on Mama. She kept repeating, 'It's not true. She couldn't have done it. It's against our religion.'

"Mama blamed those that were present when the body was brought up because she thought they had not tried hard enough to revive Granny. My aunt and uncle, who were older than Mama, seemed to take it very well. My grandfather, on the other hand, was terribly guilt-ridden all the rest of his life. He blamed himself for not hearing her get out of bed and for the well not having a locked top."

Placing, or accepting blame can become even more insidious than is related by Mary's story.

One volunteer at a suicide prevention hotline had received a call from a boy who had been badly beaten by the father of a girl who had committed suicide. The man's daughter had left a suicide note placing blame on the boy.

The father's violent reaction was an attempt to transfer some of his own feelings of guilt onto another person, but since being blamed, the boy was contemplating suicide himself. Although it is natural to want to blame someone, it is important for survivors to understand that no one is really at fault.

In the absence of open discussion and readily available information people tend to form beliefs on the basis of sketchy news reports, hearsay and offhand comments made by friends and relatives. In the following pages I will discuss some commonly held beliefs on suicide which, though they often have kernels of truth within them, are essentially myths perpetrated by a profound lack of knowledge.

These misconceptions not only hinder our knowledge about suicide, they thwart prevention and undermine the crucial support survivors need. As more information is accumulated from ongoing research, the complex issues behind the myths will become clearer, and society may begin the long process of learning to accept what they now ignore and suppress.

Take a moment now and note how many of the following statments you believe to be true.

1. People who talk about or threaten to commit suicide don't really mean it.
2. Suicides frequently occur out of the blue with no forewarning.
3. Those who commit suicide are insane.
4. Suicidal people want nothing more than to die.
5. Suicide runs in families.
6. Once a person is suicidal, he or she is suicidal forever.
7. People who try to kill themselves, but fail, won't try it again because of the shame.
8. All suicides leave a suicide note.
9. TV portrayals of suicide increase suicide among teens.
10. Cluster suicides are on the increase.
11. More suicides occur during the holidays.
12. Most suicides occur at nighttime.
13. Women threaten suicide while it is men who go through with it.
14. Celebrities are more prone to suicide than the general population.
15. Blacks and other minorities are more prone to suicide.
16. More poor and uneducated people commit suicide.
17. Religious people are less likely to commit suicide.

These myths are sweeping generalizations which have little to do with reality. They fall into four distinct categories: Basic Perceptions, Modern Media Myths, "When" Myths and "Who" myths.

MYTH #1
PEOPLE WHO TALK ABOUT (OR THREATEN) SUICIDE DON'T REALLY MEAN IT.

"Anyone who threatens suicide should be taken seriously. Approximately three-fourths of people who attempt suicide have given prior messages," says Alan L. Berman, former president of the American Association of Suicidology and currently professor of psychology at the American University in Washington, D.C.

The problem is, the signs they give aren't always clear until after the fact. "In retrospect survivors say, 'Aha, that's what it was all about.'"

Berman believes these messages are ignored for several reasons. "For the most part, what happens is that the message itself is anxiety provoking, so it is ignored as a defense against the anxiety."

"It's an awful paradox. It goes against all instincts. The survival instinct is probably the most powerful, and when someone chooses to end his life before its time, it's very distressing to us," says Sam Heilig, former executive director of the Los Angeles Suicide Prevention Center.

"A suicide makes us face the question about the meaning of our lives. Here, someone throws away his life at age twenty-four. Now what the hell does that mean?" Heilig asks.

Many times, a person has threatened suicide over and over again until it becomes the story of "The Boy Who Cried Wolf," and for this reason it is ignored.

"What happens, however, is that the person, especially a youngster, is provoked into doing something more drastic. 'Aha, now I'll really do something,' they think. Parents are often reluctant to get outside help. They feel blameworthy and they don't want to go public, so this adds to their guilt afterwards when the child attempts suicide," says Berman.

"It's different with adults. The signs may be more subtle."

Ben P. Allen, professor of psychology at Western Illinois University, says, "Ignoring a person who talks about suicide isn't the best solution. Threatening suicide should always be taken seriously. It is a deadly warning signal. There may be cases where that's all it is, but no one should make that assumption, even if it were just an attention getter. How do you ever know that?"

A counselor at a suicide prevention center recalls that a young boy who had swallowed a razor at school had previously told three of his friends what he planned to do. He asked them not to tell anyone.

"Can you imagine how they would have felt if he had been successful? He was taken to a local hospital and survived the ordeal. They didn't know what to do. They each thought they were the only person to know. That's a scary feeling," she says.

There are instances where intervention doesn't help, though. One woman whose son killed himself at age twenty-seven, and who had frequently received counseling, had been trying to kill himself since the age of five, according to his mother.

Heilig spoke of one woman in her seventiess who had tried unsuccessfully to kill herself for more than forty years. "There are simply people bent on ending their lives," says Heilig, "and treatment isn't always successful."

Still, every threat should be taken seriously because it does save lives. Just knowing that a person cares enough to take the threat seriously is meaningful to a potential suicide.

I've heard stories of people who respond to a suicide threat with anger such as, "So go ahead and kill yourself," thinking that a "get tough" attitude will jar the person out of it. I shudder to think of the consequences of such a statement. It's a bit like playing Russian Roulette.

MYTH #2
SUICIDES FREQUENTLY OCCUR OUT OF THE BLUE WITH NO FOREWARNING.

Suicides with no forewarning are extremely rare. However, it is easier to distinguish the warning signs in retrospect, especially if a person isn't familiar with them.

"Anything remotely asked about suicide shouldn't be ignored. The slightest sign shouldn't be overlooked," says professor Allen. "On the other hand, nobody can read the future. You can't be absolutely certain, and that creates a sort of dilemma."

Even if a person isn't sure, though, when certain comments or behaviors promote uneasiness, it is best to ask the person more questions about his or her feelings. It's risky to try to "talk" a person out of suicide, and if it's suspected that they are, indeed, having thoughts of suicide, professional help should be sought immediately.

Many people feel an uneasiness about talking about suicide and might be embarrassed to ask, "Are you thinking about killing yourself?" but saving a life must loom larger than any perceived embarrassment.

There is also a hesitancy sometimes to seek professional help, but overcoming the fear of going to a mental health expert is just one of the stigmas that must be eliminated if society is ever to come to grips with suicide.

Contacting the family physician can be a first step toward saving someone's life.

The most common warning signs of suicide are:

1. Suicide threats.
2. Previous suicide attempts.
3 Statements revealing a desire to die.
4. Sudden changes in behavior such as withdrawal, apathy, moodiness, anger.
5. Depression, which may manifest itself in crying, sleeplessness, loss of appetite and statements about hopelessness, helplessness and worthlessness.
6. Final arrangements, such as giving away personal possessions.
7. Sudden appearance of happiness and calmness after a period of some of the characteristics listed above.

MYTH #3
THOSE WHO COMMIT SUICIDE ARE INSANE.

"To say that someone who commits suicide is insane is a myth from a number of standpoints. Insane is a legal term. It means the person isn't legally responsible, so it's totally inappropriate. Not everyone who commits suicide is legally incompetent," says Allen.

The suicidal person clearly is not completely rational, and may not be responsible for his or her act, but this doesn't mean they are "insane."

This is not to say that a mental disorder can't trigger a suicide. Robert Cancro, M.D., professor of psychiatry at the New York University Medical Center, says that many suicides among young people are the outcome of undiagnosed schizophrenic illness.

Schizophrenics tend to attempt suicide early in their illness, and schizophrenia tends to have an earlier onset than other mental disorders.

"It is not unusual to see schizophrenic breakdowns in those between the ages of fifteen and eighteen. In fact, the bulk of such cases have broken down before the age of twenty-five," says Cancro.

Many studies indicate that diagnosed schizophrenic patients have a high rate of suicide, up to twenty times that of the normal suicide rates in the countries studied.

Manic-depressives also tend to have high suicide rates. Many turn to alcohol as a form of self-medication, according to Cancro, and since suicide is often linked to alcoholism, the problem is compounded. Alcoholism by itself may tend to promote suicide because a person who turns to it may already be depressed or have other emotional problems. It also lowers inhibitions when someone is contemplating suicide so that they may be more likely to go through with the act.

Some researchers and other mental health professionals believe that alcoholism among parents may be an even more important factor in youth suicide than alcohol abuse by young people themselves.

Alcohol and other drugs are frequently found in the blood stream of those who have committed suicide, according to Dr. Farberow. "So it serves as both a facilitator and as a reason for committing suicide. It just simply is used to provide the courage or to make it easier to carry out suicidal thoughts," he says.

Cancro has urged his colleagues in the mental health profession to be more alert to the possibility of undiagnosed schizophrenia in young persons, since it manifests itself at a time when parents may believe the teen is simply having difficulty going through adolescence. "They think the teen will outgrow it," says Cancro.

He says that parents have to learn to ignore the stigma of getting psychiatric help for their child. "Call the family physician and ask for the name of a psychiatrist knowledgeable about the disease. Parents are going to feel a lot worse if they don't get help."

A variety of treatments are used for schizophrenia, including medications, therapy, group and/or family therapy and rehabilitative techniques. Twenty percent usually recover and need no further treatment, about twenty percent need continuing treatment including medication, and the other sixty percent require treatment from time to time.

Children are particularly vulnerable to undiagnosed depression. "Kids don't articulate that they're depressed. A kid might not be conscious that he's moving toward suicide as would an adult. Their highs and lows are very different, and so they don't heed the signs," says Allen.

The incidence of depression-caused suicide is controversial. Some mental health professionals say most people who commit suicide are suffering severe depression, while others say the figure is much lower. Bem Allen states, "some researchers implicate depression in only ten percent of suicide cases." Part of the controversy may lie simply in the definition of depression. While not all suicidal people are severely depressed, it seems clear that most are in some sort of mental or emotional pain.

Wrobleski believes that the majority of people who kill themselves are "suffering from a brain disease called depression," and that there are other brain diseases such as schizophrenia that can also result in suicide. She believes, as do a great many researchers, that we inherit many things at birth, including predispositions to certain illnesses which can result in suicide.

Those who disagree call to mind the numbers of people who commit suicide in fits of anger; after violent

crimes; on impulses; and in efforts to "get even" with someone else.

Psychotherapist Carl Wold, however, believes that
suicide is violence turned inward, and that it is closely linked
with depression.

"Violent acts are committed by people who are depressed and alone and confused by their feelings and
looking for a way to express their desperation. Other modes
of communication appear blocked to them, so they move
towards violent action as a way to communicate their feelings," he explains.

"In a crisis, a violent person's alternatives seem nar-
row. They can't imagine a future."

He further states that "Machismo [an exaggerated
sense of masculinity] adds to violence and suicide because
it interferes with accepting help."

Newly incarcerated prisoners are high-risk suicides,
according to Wold, adding to the correlation between overt
acts of violence and self-destruction.

"There is a subgroup of people who commit suicide
after murders, so there has been an interest in this study.
Eight percent of all suicides begin with murder," he says.

The National Institute of Mental Health says that an
estimated fifteen percent of people who are suffering from
untreated depression take their own lives. Since approximately thirty percent of the population will suffer a severe
depressive episode in their lifetimes (unlike mild forms of
the blues that affect nearly everyone from time to time), the
seriousness of depression can't be minimized.

From nine to twenty percent of the population of all
ages in America and Europe suffer some form of depression
at any given time, according to mental health experts, but
the good news is that it's very treatable.

Because there is a growing wealth of material on
depression, which serves as both a cause and effect of

suicide (survivors also suffer from depression), and because the government has recognized the proliferation of depression in our society, there is a separate chapter in this book on the subject.

MYTH #4
SUICIDE RUNS IN FAMILIES.

Although there is no "suicide gene" for families to worry about, there *are* sociological and biological factors in families that might seem to dispose them to suicide. Statistically, a person is nine times more likely to commit suicide if he or she comes from a family with a prior suicide. It provides a role model for other family members, according to many health professionals.

What *can* be genetic is a predisposition to certain diseases that may lend themselves to suicide, such as schizophrenia, manic-depression, and possibly depression.

Researchers believe they have discovered a gene on a particular chromosome that may confer susceptibility to depression, and hence a predisposition to depressive illness, which can set the stage for suicide.

Richard T. Monahan of McLean Hospital-Harvard Medical School says more research on the biological connection is needed. "It may be more biological than we ever suspected. Certain temperaments are simply more conducive to suicide," he says.

Genetic influence on temperament is not quite the same as say, genetic influence on the height of an individual. Rather, the genes code for production of certain structures in the brain and nervous system, which in turn, affect the nervous system and hence, behavior.

Many survivors of suicide report that they feared they might take their own life following the suicide of a loved one. There seem to be some obvious reasons for this, although many factors may be involved. The first is simply that suicide has been added to their frame of reference where previously they may not have considered it. The second is that they may be gentically susceptible to depression or mental or emotional instability, and this can lead to suicidal thoughts. Finally, even if there is no initial physical predisposition towards depression, it is natural for them to be depressed about their loved one's suicide.

Clearly, there is much more research needed on this subject.

MYTH #5
SUICIDAL PEOPLE WANT NOTHING MORE THAN TO DIE.

Professionals who deal with suicide note that "Most people who attempt suicide don't really want to die. They want to end their pain." "They see no light at the end of the tunnel." "They lose all hope that it will ever get better."

"That suicidal persons want nothing more than to die is an awful myth. Suicide attempters say they don't want to die. They just want to get away from their terrible feelings," says professor of psychology Bem Allen.

"There are probably more cases of individuals who were suicidal and who don't commit suicide than those who are suicidal and go through with it. Sometimes after getting help, they are healthier and happier than ever before," Allen adds.

Michael L. Peck, former staff psychologist at the Suicide Prevention Center in Los Angeles, says it is important to recognize that for many people thoughts of suicide are temporary states of mind and that the crisis will pass.

That's why talking openly about suicide to a troubled or depressed person won't reinforce their desire to do it. They want to talk and want someone to listen — nonjudgmentally.

However, lay people should avoid giving advice and just listen. The therapy should be done by a professional.

Telling a suicidal person they have no reason to commit suicide, that life is wonderful, probably will fall on deaf ears.

Many people who attempt suicide are thankful when they are rescued, especially young children who often don't realize the finality of death. This doesn't stop them from thinking about it, however. One study found that nearly ten percent of a group of school children six to twelve years old had suicidal ideas. It is believed that these children who already have thoughts of suicide may go on to have self-destructive behaviors in adolescence and beyond.

Barry Garfinkel, an associate professor of psychiatry at the University of Minnesota School of Medicine, has said that three of every one hundred children he surveyed recently have expressed suicidal thoughts.

He also said that in a typical Minnesota high school of two thousand students, about sixty students attempt suicide every month. Often they make the attempt in their bedrooms and then sleep it off without telling anyone.

Some researchers speculate that the reason so many youths attempt suicide in the evening hours is because someone will be around to save them. They don't really want to die.

"When we ask kids, 'Did you really mean to kill yourself?' they frequently answer, 'I don't know,'" says Monahan.

Peck says that most adolescents who are suicidal tell a friend. "They don't tell a teacher. They don't tell a counselor or parents. They tell a friend first, usually a classmate. We found that twenty-five to thirty percent of all tenth grade students in a survey had had a friend tell them about a planned suicide. When you go into the classroom and ask for a show of hands on 'How many of you have had a friend tell you,' you'd be amazed. So the idea is to educate them as to what to do. How to handle it. How to know when their friend says not to tell anybody, that they don't pay any attention to that."

Again, it is important to just listen to a potential suicide and not offer advice except to suggest that they seek professional help. And when a youth confides an intent to commit suicide to a friend, the friend should tell a school official or the parents. The parents should get professional help immediately.

The sister of a young man who committed suicide recalls that the night before he committed suicide he called and began talking about his problems. "I just didn't have time to listen. At the time I had so many problems of my own I didn't think I could handle any more," she recalls. "Now I have to live with that. If only I had taken the time to listen."

MYTH #6
ONCE A PERSON IS SUICIDAL, HE OR SHE IS SUICIDAL FOREVER.

Very few people who attempt suicide really want to die, and if intervention is achieved and the person receives adequate help and counseling, they go on to a much better life wondering why they ever tried it in the first place.

The crisis is usually temporary, according to most researchers, and following a suicide attempt that is thwarted, the people (usually after hospitalization and counseling) are thankful for being saved.

In fact, nine out of ten people who attempt suicide never try it again.

MYTH #7
PEOPLE WHO TRY TO KILL THEMSELVES, BUT FAIL, WON'T TRY AGAIN BECAUSE OF THE SHAME.

Although the statistic cited above indicates that most will not attempt suicide a second time, the danger is very real because people who are still suicidal will keep trying.

Once a person has attempted suicide, the next time becomes easier because they've crossed a major barrier. It's like getting up the courage to try something new that seems insurmountable and finding that it wasn't so difficult after all. For every five people who commit suicide, four have made previous attempts.

Another point of consideration is that suicidal people who are hospitalized receive constant care. Once they are released from the hospital, this intensive care and attention is taken from them, and they are left without the strong social support they had been receiving.

Farberow points out that in the late fifties and early sixties it was found that when patients were discharged from the hospitals in great numbers due to the increasing use of psychotropic drugs, the suicide rate increased because they lacked the social, intimate support they had previously been getting.

MYTH #8
ALL SUICIDES LEAVE A SUICIDE NOTE.

Fewer than one-quarter of suicides leave notes and then they're usually garbled. Often the explanations they give for their suicide aren't the true reasons — only what they believe to be true in their particular states of mind.

It must be remembered that all suicide isn't the result of depression or mental illness. Barrett points out that some suicides act on impulse out of anger and revenge. And if someone leaves a suicide note acting out of revenge, the results can be devastating to the survivor.

Edwin Shneidman, noted American expert on suicide, writes in *Voices of Death,* "In order to commit suicide, one cannot write a meaningful suicide note; conversely, if one could write a meaningful note, one would not have to commit suicide...Life is like a long letter and the suicide note is merely a postscript to it and cannot, by itself, be expected to carry the burden of substituting for the total document."

The next two beliefs represent what I call modern media myths, and have been the topic of a great deal of discussion in recent years.

MYTH #9
TV PORTRAYALS OF SUICIDE INCREASE SUICIDE AMONG TEENS.

In 1987 much publicized reports indicated that TV portrayals of suicide increased the risk of suicide among teens.

This was later refuted in articles in the *New England Journal of Medicine,* but there is still controversy surrounding the issue.

The original reports were based on a widely publicized paper by David Shaffer, M.D. and Marilyn Gould, Ph.D. which appeared in the *New England Journal of Medicine* in 1986.

In 1987 in the same journal, sociologist David Phillips reported that he had tried and failed to replicate the 1986 study. Gould and Shaffer then acknowledged in another article appearing in *Suicide & Life-Threatening Behavior,* that fictional stories featuring suicidal behavior appear less widespread than had originally been proposed.

What may be true, according to Phillips, is that nonfictional portrayals increase suicides, but that fictional portrayals don't.

But in another study, Berman found no evidence of increased suicides after TV portrayals of suicide, and Ronald Kessler, Ph.D. reported in the November, 1988 issue of the *American Journal of Psychiatry* that during 1981-84 teenage suicides decreased after newscasts about suicide.

Phillips also says that it's unclear whether or not education about suicide leads to more of it.

"A lot of the people who are interested in educational programs are very upset about the materials showing that it may increase suicide. As Americans we would like to believe, as everyone would, that educational programs have a positive effect. I haven't seen it proven and the studies are inconclusive," says Phillips.

But many professionals believe that not providing education and not talking openly about suicide increases the risk. In a McNeill-Lehrer News Report on PBS in 1987 Shneidman likened suicide education to AIDS education, noting that prevention is nearly impossible without it.

Allen believes that while showing suicide on TV may not play a direct role in increasing suicide, it may play an indirect role by desensitizing the act.

"It's similar to the violence on TV. It desensitizes people. It tends to trivialize suicide. It's no longer a big deal."

MYTH #10
CLUSTER SUICIDES ARE ON THE INCREASE.

The term cluster suicide generally refers to two or more people, sometimes acquaintances, who commit suicide at the same time, or within the same community or school. Cluster suicides are quite rare and there's not a great deal of hard research on the subject, although there is a lot of speculation as to the causes.

According to Patrick O'Carroll, M.D. of the Center for Disease Control in Atlanta, Georgia, there is no standard definition of cluster suicides in existence. It is sometimes called "copycat" suicide.

However, in order to put cluster suicides in perspective, perhaps two hundred youth have killed themselves in what could be termed cluster suicides, while more than ten thousand annually do it in singular fashion. Cluster suicides make news. Singular events don't.

Wrobleski also points out an elitist connection to cluster suicides. She writes, "The talk about imitation and contagion began when the first so-called 'cluster' suicides occurred in Plano, Texas and Westchester County, New York. It may be that in the cluster suicides we saw what had been happening all along; random statistical groupings of suicides that were selectively noticed. There was a cluster in North Dakota and one in Wisconsin, but they never received months and years of publicity. The clusters in prosperous Plano and wealthy Westchester County did receive sustained attention.

"It isn't that children from well-to-do families had not killed themselves before, but that the taboo had lifted enough so there was a large outcry from the parents in those upper middle class communities. The cry went up that, 'Now it is our children, and we won't stand for it.' It's analogous to the time years ago when drugs reached the suburbs. It was not that it was new, but that it was now affecting large numbers of people who could demand action."

When "cluster suicide" does occur, one contributing factor might be that teens are particularly vulnerable because they can't stand the thought of losing a confident — a best friend. Allen links this theory to a feeling of rootlessness, fostered by the mobility of today's families. Children often don't stay in one place long enough to develop lasting friendships, and losing one that has been developed can be more than the young person can bear.

The next two myths are what I call the "when" myths.

MYTH #11
MOST SUICIDES OCCUR AT NIGHTTIME.

Night seems to cloak everything, but suicides occur at every hour of the day and night.

Actually more suicides occur in the spring and late summer when daylight is extended.

The British Journal of Psychiatry reports that "the pre-summer peak in suicide reflects the hope among the unhappy and the lonely that the end of winter will bring an end to the social isolation and depression brought about by the cold weather. Spring comes but leaves matters unchanged.

"The post-summer peak in suicide may result from the realization that the spring and summer did not bring about a change in life circumstances and the resultant feelings of hopelessness."

"Spring is a transition season when things change very rapidly," observed the late Helmut Landsberg, a meteorologist at the University of Maryland. "This change in light seems to affect human glands and internal reactions."

Dr. Michael Gauquelin, a French psychologist, in his book *How Atmospheric Conditions Affect Your Health,* writes that "Spring is a period when new romances start, when fresh plans are made...but it is also a season when people experience frequent changes of mood and have bitter arguments with one another."

And German studies in the 1960s said that "Spring may well be the season for all forms of impulsive behavior."

The U.S. Centers for Disease Control found that between 1969 and 1978, "The suicide pattern was distinctly seasonal, above average all spring and below average all winter."

Other researchers have found that youths tend to commit more suicide during the spring, especially in March. It is speculated that children are vulnerable in the spring because it is a period of hope and rebirth, which can be intolerable to a child in despair.

Also, "Blue Monday" is not a misnomer. Research indicates that people are most likely to attempt suicide on Mondays.

MYTH #12
MORE SUICIDES OCCUR DURING THE HOLIDAYS.

Despite the message of "holiday blues" beamed across the media during the Christmas holidays, suicides actually go down during this season. Actually, so does serious depression.

Statistics compiled by Phillips show suicides are down during most of our major holidays, including Christmas. Three other holidays, New Year's Day, the Fourth of July and Labor Day, however, register increases in suicide.

Phillips believes that because Christmas and Thanksgiving are family celebrations, they might have a protective effect.

Suicide hotlines receive fewer calls during Christmas holidays and during the World Series and special events such as the Olympics and during catastrophes such as earthquakes.

"Celebrations and rituals, no matter how insignificant they appear, are heavy with meaning. They provide roots and foster a deeper sense of purpose and meaning in our lives," says Carlfred Broderick, a University of Southern California sociologist and psychologist.

Psychiatrist Dr. Walter Brackelmans agrees. "Rituals tend to represent, symbolically, a connectedness for family members. They get a clear account of their own identity. When families, or individuals are in trouble, one of the first things to go is the ritual celebration. The connecting structure is fractured," he says.

"We should celebrate every chance we get because life is tough," adds Broderick.

The following "who" myths are not true, as we know that men and women of all classes and races commit suicide. "Everyone has the potential for committing suicide," says Santa Monica psychologist Carl Wold.

MYTH #13
WOMEN THREATEN SUICIDE WHILE IT IS MEN WHO GO THROUGH WITH IT.

It is true that more men than women kill themselves. What doesn't appear to be true is that women don't really mean it when they attempt.

Four times as many women attempt suicide as men. Men are more successful at suicide partly because they use more violent, direct methods. Men tend to either shoot or hang themselves, while women try pills (that often aren't successful) and carbon monoxide poisoning.

This is changing, however. The U.S. Centers for Disease Control report that in 1970 less than one-third of the suicides by women aged fifteen to twenty-four were with a gun. Forty-two percent of those who killed themselves used drugs. By 1984 the percentage using drugs had dropped to nineteen percent and those using guns had increased to fifty percent.

The change, according to some researchers, is because barbituates, frequently used to commit suicide, are now more difficult to obtain, whereas it's easy to get a gun.

MYTH #14
CELEBRITIES ARE MORE PRONE TO SUICIDE THAN THE GENERAL POPULATION.

Celebrities are no more likely to commit suicide than anyone else, according to many researchers. It may seem they do, but that's because their names make headlines.

"It's the media that gives us the impression that they are more prone. For a long time, the media wouldn't print suicides, especially when it was a youth, but that has changed, and it's good. Suicide needs to be made public so that others will be more aware of what is happening," says Allen.

Traditionally, newsrooms have had a policy of printing only the suicides of notables, or if the suicide took place in an unusual setting or circumstance. Sometimes the media cannot obtain information anyway, because most police departments won't release the names of suicide victims in efforts to protect the families, or to avoid lawsuits.

It may be that if celebrities talk about their own thoughts of suicide, or speak out when other notables take their own lives, they can help shatter some of the myths surrounding suicide. They can let the public know that suicide isn't something to hide in the closet, and that a greater proportion of the population has considered it than we ever realized.

When someone like Sid Caesar acknowledges that he has had thoughts of suicide, or when a seemingly gentle man like Iron Eyes Cody, cast as the crying indian for environmental commercials, talks about his thoughts of suicide, it makes us realize that suicide is a stranger to no one.

Cody says that after his wife died he returned to his lonely Montana cabin where "Gray Eagle" had been filmed and tried to commit suicide. He took some pills and lay by the lake in his sleeping bag thinking he would never wake up. That is, until some geese began biting him.

Later, he tried to run his white Cadillac off a mountain road, but that too failed.

MYTH #15
BLACKS AND OTHER MINORITIES ARE MORE PRONE TO SUICIDE.

The exact opposite is true. Blacks have one of the lowest suicide rates in the United States.

A black man being interviewed on TV once said, "Blacks don't commit suicide like the rest of the population because we've learned to live with the blues throughout our entire lives."

And comedian Dick Gregory once said, "You can't kill yourself by jumping out of the basement."

Dr. Richard J. Seiden, professor of behavioral sciences at the University of California at Berkeley, says the rest of the population can learn from the coping style of blacks.

"I'm not saying people should live in poverty and suffer from discrimination, but it seems the people with the most to live for seemingly, which is white males, have the hardest road. I have the feeling that one of the variables is how much you aspire to. I think a lot of people are very unhappy because of the standards they set for themselves. They are frustrated. We need to look at the coping skills developed by minorities to learn to adapt to these frustrations.

"I've found that in studies of students who kill themselves, one of the first hypotheses to be put forth is that they must be doing terrible in school, but it has turned out to be the opposite. Students who kill themselves have all sorts of honors and higher grades, but have an internal feeling of not being happy with themselves," says Seiden.

On the other hand, researchers are finding that black college students, and women (of all races), are *becoming* more like white males in terms of suicide. "It really isn't a racial difference in the genes. It is a class system. We find it all over the world. People in the upper classes all over have a higher suicide rate. Even studies done in the armed forces show that white collar workers have higher rates than blue collar workers.

"As more blacks become involved in the American Dream — that is, material success — their suicide rates increase," says Seiden.

Along with material success comes increased suicide rates among the elderly of various cultures.

In non-industrialized countries, suicide rates among the old are extremely low. As countries become modernized and industrialized, they're no longer interested in the wisdom of the elders. Since the old are no longer valued, their suicide rates begin to increase. It's a matter of feeling useless, worn out and isolated, according to Seiden. (Other factors, such as the pain of cancer or other illnesses also contribute).

"In minority communities, there isn't enough money to hire help to take care of the children and to prepare all the meals, so the elderly are needed. In affluent families, they can hire [help] and send the old to homes," says Seiden.

Interestingly, although the suicide rate among old people is higher than for any other age group, it is declining.

Seiden links this decline to the increased political power of the elderly. It gives them the idea that they can do something to change their lives and have more control over it. "Suicide comes from a feeling of helplessness that nothing can be done. That's how people think before they kill themselves."

MYTH #16
MORE POOR AND UNEDUCATED PEOPLE COMMIT SUICIDE.

"It's a misconception that more bad things happen to poor people. Money has nothing to do with it," says Allen. Suicide crosses all socioeconomic barriers.

Suicide is the leading killer of physicians graduating from John Hopkins Medical School. Also, the suicide rate for female physicians is four times higher than for women in other walks of life, according to 1984 research.

Psychologist Michael Peck says that college students who commit suicide tend to come from intact middle-class families and to be average students. They aren't neurotic, nor do they have problems with grades in school.

Javad H. Kashani, M.D., professor of psychiatry, reported in the *American Journal of Psychiatry* that one-fourth of college freshmen will consider suicide. Suicide is the second leading cause of death among college-aged people. He believes it is caused from the pressure of coming from childhood to young adulthood, and the pressure to do well academically. The stress leads to depression and is often accompanied by abusing alcohol or drugs.

It is true, according to Peck, that the non-student rate of suicide among youths of college age is actually two to three times higher than that of college students, but this isn't necessarily linked to economic factors.

MYTH #17
RELIGIOUS PEOPLE ARE LESS LIKELY TO COMMIT SUICIDE.

What once may have been true is no longer. People of all religious faiths commit suicide. During the time when the Catholic Church held sway in Europe, suicide was practically unknown, and when it did occur, it was covered up by the family. The stigma was just too much to bear.

During the Middle Ages, it was believed that few persons of any faith committed suicide, except for sporadic outbursts of mass suicide among Jews when persecution reached horrendous intensity.

However, some religious leaders today say that because of the oppressive conditions during that period, and the hideous conditions that existed for the survivors, it was pretty much covered up. That, in fact, a great many individual suicides did occur.

Jewish laws among pious Jews have, in the past, resulted in very low suicide rates. Although the Jewish suicide rate is increasing, it is still lower than for other religions.

There are no specific laws in the Bible against suicide. It wasn't until the fifth century A.D. that laws were invoked by church leaders based on the Commandment: "Thou shalt not kill."

6

CONFRONTING DEPRESSION

D<small>EPRESSION</small> effects people in all cultures and doesn't discriminate as to race, creed or socioeconomic factors.

It's been the target of extensive research throughout the ages, and was thought by the ancient Greeks to be caused by the presence of black bile in the bloodstream. Hippocrates described it as melancholia.

The Menninger Foundation in Topeka, Kansas, which is dedicated to advancing the cause of good mental health, offers these little-known words of Abraham Lincoln on depression in *Menninger Perspective*: "I am now the most miserable man living. If what I feel were equally distributed to the whole human family, there would not be one cheerful face on earth. Whether I shall ever be better, I cannot tell; I awfully forbode I shall not. To remain as I am is impossible. I must die or be better, it appears to me."

Whatever the label given depression, and whatever the underlying reasons for being depressed (and there are many), it's been recognized as a major health problem that can lead to suicide.

The National Institute of Mental Health considers depression so debilitating to the nation that it has launched a major campaign to enlighten physicians, mental health professionals and the public about this major health problem that affects twenty-five percent of all women and twelve percent of all men during their lifetimes, and costs the economy an estimated sixteen billion dollars annually.

They hope to bring it out of the dark ages by getting people to recognize that traditional methods of diagnosis and treatment haven't been as effective as needed, and to suggest new methods through a program called D/ART (Depression/Awareness, Recognition, Treatment).

They also state that depression may be associated with biological disturbances, which could be a result of genetic factors or environmental factors.

NIMH's program disseminates information on how to recognize depression with new tests that analyze brain waves and the chemical content of blood and urine. It also recommends what it believes are some of the most effective methods of treatment. This sometimes includes short-term use of medication to get the person's brain chemicals in balance before and during therapy. This method can produce normal functioning within weeks, rather than the several months or years it can take with traditional methods.

Presently, most physicians rely on family histories, physical examinations and questions and answers to help diagnose depression, but the new laboratory tests are far more accurate and speedy, according to Anne Rosenfeld of NIMH.

Many researchers believe that depression in the United States is an epidemic, and they note that a large percentage of the thirty thousand suicides that occur annually in the United States happen to people who are clinically depressed.

"Clinically depressed," means that a depressed person

has a certain collection of symptoms that last more than two weeks.

Many of us suffer short periods of depression and some will have only one episode in a lifetime. Others have them periodically, and in some cases, depression is present most of the time.

Some mental health professionals say that children as young as five suffer from depression, but their symptoms are difficult to recognize. Adolescent depression is on the increase, and suicide is the second leading cause of death among fifteen to twenty-four-year olds.

Usually, however, the first episode of depression is most likely to strike women in their late thirties and men in their late forties. More than one million Americans past age sixty-five suffer clinical depression. Often it is diagnosed as senility.

It was once believed that menopausal women were more susceptible to depression, but it has been shown that depression actually decreases among women between the ages of forty-five and sixty, according to several studies.

In addition to regular depressive moods, short-term or clinical depression, there are more serious manifestations of depressions. NIMH says that at least one million people experience cycles of terrible "lows" and inappropriate "highs." This emotional roller coaster is called manic-depressive disorder or "bipolar" depression. Its symptoms include inappropriate elation; grandiose notions; increased talking, moving and sexual activity; racing thoughts; disturbed ability to make decisions; and disturbed social behaviors.

The symptoms of depression are:

1. Persistent sad, anxious, or "empty" mood.
2. Feelings of hopelessness, pessimism.
3. Feelings of guilt, worthlessness, helplessness.
4. Loss of interest or pleasure in ordinary activities, including sex.
5. Sleep disturbances (insomnia, early-morning waking, or oversleeping).
6. Eating disturbances (either loss or gain of appetite and weight).
7. Decreased energy, fatigue, being "slowed down."
8. Thoughts of death or suicide, suicide attempts.
9. Restlessness, irritability.
10. Difficulty concentrating, remembering, making decisions.
11. Physical symptoms, such as headaches, digestive disorder, and chronic pain that do not respond to treatment.

If more than four of these symptoms are present, seek help through a physician, mental health specialist, health maintenance organization, community mental health center, a state hospital, outpatient clinic, private clinic or a family service agency.

The sad fact is, most people don't get proper treatment for any type of depression, either because they aren't aware of their symptoms, they've been misdiagnosed, or because they are engulfed in thoughts of the social stigma of "going to a shrink."

It is perplexing to those of us concerned about depression, that people refuse to get treatment when their lives can be made so much richer by eliminating the cloud of depression.

Therapy no longer consists of lying on a couch talking about your problems infinitely.

Eighty percent of people with serious depression can be treated successfully. Medication or psychological therapies, or combinations of both usually relieve symptoms in weeks, and often in the new therapies, half of the people with major depression can be completely free of symptoms in four to eight months.

Even the most severe forms of depression can respond rapidly to treatment.

Research supported by grants from the NIMH, the Alcohol, Drug Abuse and Mental Health Administration, the Public Health Service and the US Department of Health and Human Services, documents recent trends in depression, some of which were reported by Gerald L. Klerman, M.D. in the *British Journal of Psychiatry*, 1988.

These trends include:

An increase in depression since World War II.
An increase in depression, suicide and drug
    abuse among those born after World War II,
    commonly referred to as the "Baby Boom
    Generation."
Depression beginning at an earlier age.
An apparent decrease in depression among those
    over sixty.
Increased depression among females.

Recently developed objective laboratory tests are used in diagnosing depression. Measurement of hormones and brain chemicals found in blood, urine and spinal fluid give clues to treatment selection, including when to begin medication and when to stop.

Many researchers believe that some people have a physical predisposition to depression, and that biochemical factors coupled with stressful life events can trigger depression.

According to information from the Neurosciences Information Center, a professional service of the Upjohn Company, a single cause, or a combination of factors, can create depression.

These factors include:

1. Depletion of brain cell transmitter substances: There is growing evidence that some depressions result from abnormalities in communication among brain cells caused by insufficient amounts of norepinephrine and serotonin.

2. Loss, crisis, or a major life change. It is normal for these events to trigger short-term depression. Sometimes, however, they can trigger long-lasting depression which needs treatment.

3. Anger turned inward: This is the classic psychoanalytic description of depression. Some psychologists have observed that women tend to respond to adversity by blaming themselves while men tend to blame the world outside them. Some offer these tendencies to explain the higher incidence of depression in women.

4. Drugs: The side effects of alcohol, barbiturates, narcotics, corticosteroids, certain antihypertensives and oral contraceptives may include depression.

5. Disease: Obviously, illness can bring on de-

pression. The likelihood is greatest with arthritis, heart disease, hypothyroidism and cancer.

The Center also reports that "although unipolar [symptoms of depression only] and bipolar [extreme highs and lows] depressions seem to run in families, no recognizable pattern of inheritance has been found. Nonetheless, scientists, using new techniques for manipulating DNA, are actively searching for a depression gene."

"Researchers at the University of Rochester believe they have identified such a gene. Studying families in which two or more members suffer major depressive episodes, researchers found one particular gene more common among affected members. How the gene increases susceptibility to depression is not known. Genetic studies have potential value in predicting persons at high risk for depressive disorder.

"The most promising area is the development of more and better tests which not only diagnose depression but also distinguish among types. Tests now in use include measurements for irregularities in the production of cortisol, thyroxin and growth hormones. The mechanisms relating these to depression are not known.

The center cautions that "It cannot be said with certainty that heredity is the cause of depressive symptoms. In the classic chicken-and egg dilemma, it's possible that trauma and subsequent depression produce some of the physiological changes."

Neurotransmitters are the chemical messengers of the nervous system responsible for communication between nerve cells or neurons. Certain neurotransmitters, such as norepinephrine, act as the brain's thermostats, working to regulate other brain regions throughout the central nervous system. Norepinephrine plays a modulatory role in the brain and seems to be of importance in the control of mood.

Other causes of depression can be physical illnesses, certain medications and abnormal hormonal systems. However, this can also be a "chicken or the egg" question, as it is not known whether physical problems cause depression or depression causes physical problems (or both).

Researchers at Washington University School of Medicine in St. Louis say that clinical depression may be as big a risk factor in coronary artery disease (CAD) as cigarette smoking, elevated cholesterol or high blood pressure.

Robert Carney, Ph.D., associate professor of psychology at Washington University, found that nearly one out of five CAD patients had had documented incidences of clinical depression *prior* to their CAD diagnosis, and in the year *following* their diagnosis, these patients were twice as likely as non-depressed patients to have a major coronary event such as heart attack, surgery or death.

Physicians have traditionally believed that depression is a normal reaction to being diagnosed with CAD. Twenty to sixty percent of CAD patients are depressed at some time during the course of their illness.

"The first step is to identify the depression and that tends not to be done in patients who have a medical illness. Studies suggest that two-thirds of people who have a psychiatric disorder on top of a medical disorder go unnoticed and untreated," says Carney.

"There is clearly a mind-body problem in much of medicine and there are major physiological changes that result when people are depressed," he adds.

Some researchers think depression may affect the body to such an extent that it causes irregular heart rhythms or the progression of arteriosclerosis. Others suggest that depression might adversely affect motivation, and people stop doing the things that keep their bodies healthy, according to Carney.

Some people respond to drug therapy, some to psychological treatment and others to both.

Two types of therapies are emerging as the treatments of choice by a growing number of patients suffering from depression. Neither requires lengthy, traditional analytic approaches, and both have been scrutinized by NIMH. These treatments may be used in conjunction with medication, depending on the severity of the depression.

Both of these therapies deal with the "here and now," and don't place emphasis on delving into the person's past.

One is "interpersonal psychotherapy," or IPT, which holds the view that depression is usually associated with the disruption of intimate relationships.

Interpersonal psychotherapy involves itself with four types of problems lending themselves to depression. One is abnormally severe grief reactions over the death of a loved one. Another is the interpersonal deficits involving socially isolated people. A third is interpersonal disputes caused by poor communication, and a fourth is role transitions, created with life changes such as switching jobs or "empty nest syndrome."

Studies of interpersonal psychotherapy indicate that women suffer more depression than men because they place a higher value on intimate relationships.

Gerald Klerman, M.D., a psychiatrist at Cornell University, and a pioneer in developing interpersonal psychotherapy, says that depressed people, and this can include survivors of suicide, need help in dealing with unresolved grief.

"It's made more difficult for the survivor because of the stigma that's attached to suicide in our society and in most other societies," he says. The focus for the survivor is to learn to get on with life, according to Klerman.

"There is no blame for suicide. I'm not interested in blaming people. This isn't a moral judgment. We're interested in helping people cope better with their problems."

Cognitive therapy, the other emerging treatment of choice for depression, deals more with a person's own thought patterns, rather than relationships.

Psychotherapist Gary Emery, a pioneer in cognitive therapy and author of several books on the subject, including *Getting Undepressed, Own Your Own Life,* and *A New Beginning,* says that basically, cognitive therapy emphasizes that depression stems from self-destructive, pessimistic patterns of thinking that usually develop over a lifetime. Patients are made aware of these patterns, and new ways of changing the distorted thinking that lies at the heart of the problem are instilled.

Cognitive therapy holds the view that the depressed person has a negative view of the self, the world and the future.

"It's a self-help technique that focuses on the vicious cycle of negative thinking such as, 'If I'm not on top, I'm a flop,'" according to Emery.

"Researchers know what depression is. It is a clear-cut thing that can be measured," says Emery. "Depressed people tend to blame themselves rather than others, or the environment, for their troubles, and to personalize the problems — 'It's my fault because...' — rather than treating it objectively," he says.

Women tend to heap more blame on themselves and they underestimate their ability to control a situation, he believes.

"Men, on the other hand, tend to blame others for faults, and overestimate their ability to handle situations."

Emery's latest book, *Rapid Relief From Emotional*

Distress, written with James Campbell, M.D., is a speeded up version of cognitive therapy.

Emery said the methods described are helpful for eighty percent of depressed people, with the other twenty percent needing longer term types of therapy.

"This twenty percent seem to have trouble really listening, or hearing. They are so involved in their own thoughts that they can't take in other ideas. It's kind of like a habit. Their depression is a lifetime habit — a failure to develop emotionally.

"Mainly what cognitive therapy does is get you to stop thinking about your problems. Get the focus off yourself. Off your concerns."

Cognitive therapy can be used for survivors of suicide. "At first survivors really aren't in a state of mind where they can make sense of the situation," says Emery. At this stage, which may wax and wane for some time, there may be no need for therapy because grief and depression are normal reactions to the loss. But Emery believes survivors need to refocus their thoughts once they're past the initial stages of grief. To this end, Emery disagrees with some professionals who say survivors need to ventilate their feelings. "I really think the main thing is not to continually think about the situation. Maybe initially it helps, but after that it's not good. It only stimulates the negative feelings," Emery says.

He adds that it's "unhealthy" for someone to be grieving several years after the suicide, and that if it's caused by guilt, they should remove it, the same as other negative emotions.

"People sort of believe they should feel guilty. It's not necessary or useful. It doesn't help anybody. These [guilty] thoughts are really like behavior. If you don't reinforce them, they won't come back. If they keep coming back, it's because the person is attending to them.

"The other thing is, when the thoughts come through,

they are just thoughts. The reality is that the [suicide] is bigger than any of your thoughts. So you might think, 'I wasn't the best parent.' There may be a kernel of truth to that, but the real truth is, it's too big to explain just by thought. You can never get to any real causes. There is no solution to your thinking. People really have to learn to let go of their negative thinking," says Emery.

Cognitive approaches are also being used to deal with stress, which often precipitates depression. A National Academy of Sciences study found that many cognitive approaches increase a person's knowledge about, and sense of control over, a stressful situation and are more effective than other techniques.

Cognitive approaches are, in some ways, similar to Morita Therapy, a Japanese discipline which is being used by a growing number of therapists in the United States. Morita therapy emphasizes physical and mental action to overcome psychological problems. It is part of an overall program called "constructive living."

David K. Reynolds, Ph.D., trained in anthropology and one of the pioneers of Morita Therapy in the United States, says that one of the general principals of the therapy is the basic notion that, "the feelings of anguish, rage and abandonment that survivors of suicide have are natural and don't need to be fixed."

"The strategy is to accept feelings as they come up, and there is no need to work on them, which is a little different than the Western tradition of trying to 'fix' all feeling.

"One can expect [the feelings] to fade as time passes. That is the natural condition, provided over time that things don't come up to restimulate them. We recommend that once the initial grieving is over and they have talked about the experience and how awful it was, then we don't recommend they spend a lot of time restimulating the feelings by talking about them. One is to get on with one's life.

"This initial period of grieving varies from person to person.

"This concept really isn't hard for Western culture to accept. Once they start living this way, it makes a lot of sense and there is a lot of relief that they don't have to go over and over it. The repeated going over and over creates a mental rut that doesn't seem to help anything, and it makes them more miserable."

Reynolds explains that temporary relief from mental anguish can result from some sort of action such as washing dishes. "I've been distracted temporarily, and when I finish washing the dishes, behold, they are clean. So we recommend physical distraction, but that is an initial step. The next step is an acceptance of the suicide. Distraction is still a kind of running away. The goal isn't to bring the survivor back up to some "normal" state, which is the goal of Western culture — to get them as close as they can be to what they were before. In constructive living, that isn't the goal at all. It's to help them go beyond what they knew before and to be alive and above the suffering. They grow beyond what they were before.

"There will come a time, for a lot of students, when they say something like, 'I'm sorry I had to go through that awful experience, but I'm glad that it prompted me to be in touch with other things and to learn this principal because I'm a lot richer now.'

"People in touch with grief become better people," says Reynolds.

"Nobody really comes to terms with grief, and understanding that is just practical common sense. It is basically human nature."

Reynolds believes that Eastern culture is creeping into the West because more Asians are living here and we're getting better translations of Asian reading materials.

As we adopt some Eastern traditions, so are the Japanese and Chinese adopting some of Western culture. Both Eastern and Western are developing more leisure time, and with that comes more choice on how to spend that time. "Previously, people didn't have much time to grieve. They had to get back to work in order to survive. They felt the hurt just as much, but they had to get on with everyday living."

Constructive living is also composed of Naikan, as well as Morita Therapy. Naikan is a strategy that aims at helping us look at how we're supported by the world all the time in practical things. "For example," says Reynolds, "This conversation is made possible by thousands of people. We don't know all their names, yet somebody at the telephone company is helping. Somebody taught us how to use the language we're using. Somebody went to the trouble to educate us for the skills we have. And two people gave me this body. So I don't have to look at life in some abstract, philosophical way.

"I have to conclude, if I've got my eyes open, that any time I think I'm a self-made man, I'm conning myself. Even the slightest thing is a gift. For example, the clothes I'm wearing, I didn't make. Somebody grew cotton. Somebody made it. I bought it somewhere. Then I wonder where the money came from to buy it. It came from somebody who gave it to me. They say I earned that money, but who taught me to earn it?

"So when I start looking at the details of anything that's mine, it turns out to be a kind of gift. Naikan is a practice that helps one look concretely at the support, not only of other people, but of things. So we're continually being supported by the world.

"This is a useful concept for those who are suffering because they tend to become self-centered," says Reynolds.

There are dozens of types of therapies that can be

used to help people suffering from depression, and if a person doesn't feel the therapy or therapist is helping, they should consult another.

Any person suffering from depression, including survivors of suicide, should also consult a physician, however. Many physical conditions can cause depression, such as viral infections, cancer, head injuries, autoimmune diseases and diseases of the thyroid, adrenal or pituitary gland.

Many drugs can also cause depression such as steroids, birth control pills, hypertension medications and combinations of certain drugs.

Survivors of suicide need to recognize if their grief reaction is "normal" or if it is in danger of becoming a serious depression. Many survivors say their greatest help came from taking part in survivors of suicide support groups. A listing of these support groups as well as a listing of crisis centers where help is available for those suffering from depression is provided in the back of the book.

Adina Wrobleski, a suicidologist and a survivor notes, "I think it may be a matter of expectations. If a suicide survivor, who is deeply vulnerable immediately following the death, is told that he or she has a 'very serious problem that can have dire consequences for the rest of your life,' this expectation may well be fulfilled. Conversely, if this vulnerable person is told that, 'Yes, this is an awful and tragic thing, but others have been through this experience and come out well, and you can too,' there exists an expectation that can also be fulfilled. The key may be the message suicide survivors hear in this crucial period."

7

PREVENTING SUICIDE

THE FOLLOWING letter, a cry for help, was sent to me after a series of articles I wrote on suicide appeared in a Los Angeles area newspaper. The fifteen-year-old girl who wrote it indicated she had contacted a crisis center in her area, which can be a first line of defense in the prevention of suicide. However, I was never able to respond because no address had been provided for return and other methods of locating her failed. She wrote, "There are many things to prevent suicide. If people did not have troubles they would not need suicide. I have thought of it many times because of not having someone to talk to. So all I did was called the Suicide Prevention and it helped me a lot.

"I am fifteen years old. My problems all start with my parents. Me and my parents get along but sometimes they tell me not to do something and I do anyway. I understand why they get mad at me then. Sometimes they get mad at me because they are mad at someone else.

"I have an older brother and an older sister and a younger sister, so I am just pushed away.

"If you have an answer to this please write me back."

The majority of mental health experts say that most suicidal people give warning signals. These signs, however, often don't register on our conscious minds until after the fact — then it's too late. Even when hints are given most people are hesitant to broach the subject or to ask the direct question, "Are you thinking of committing suicide?" Those words aren't in our lexicon.

There is also a growing body of research suggesting that people who are intent on committing suicide can't be simply talked out of it. Statistics indicate that counties providing hotlines continue to have suicide rates matching those that don't.

Caution must be used, however, when dealing with statistics. They don't paint the entire picture.

For one thing, most agencies with suicide hotlines are relatively new to the communities they are serving. Hotlines are generally associated with prevention centers that are doing many other types of outreach. At the onset as these centers establish themselves, there is a greater awareness filling the community, including closer involvement with the coroner's office. Typically, more suicides, more people in crisis, and additional people in high-risk groups begin utilizing the services of the center.

Because of the added awareness of suicide in these communities, more suicides are reported, where before, they may have been covered up or overlooked. In other words, suicides are being prevented, but at the same time more of them previously hidden in the closet are being reported.

It may take several years for a community that has recently become involved with suicide prevention to show lowered statistics.

In the meantime, lives are being saved, counseling is made available to families in crisis, and the general atmosphere of the community is one of actively working to make life better for its residents.

Los Angeles, where the first suicide prevention center in the country was established nearly thirty years ago, is a prime example.

Co-director of that center, Dr. Norman L. Farberow, a pioneer in suicide prevention research, and co-author with Glenn Evans of the *Encyclopedia of Suicide,* says that Los Angeles, and California in general, have typically had high suicide rates, as do most sun-belt states. The incidence of suicide in these states remain higher than others partly due to the presence of large populations of elderly people who have the highest suicide rate of any age group (age 65 to 74 is about 19 per 100,000 and age 75 to 84 is about 29 per 100,000, compared to about 13 per 100,000 for the general population).

Nevertheless, a few years after the center was established in Los Angeles, the rates began declining. As an example, by 1970, there were about one thousand reported suicide deaths in Los Angeles, down from an average of fourteen hundred in previous years. The declining figure was parallel throughout the state, which had followed the example of Los Angeles in establishing prevention centers up and down the coast. "In other words, we're bombarded with education and training, and it's effective. It may simply take a while for these newer centers and hotlines to get entrenched," says Farberow.

Not all suicides can be prevented, but if the life of one person is saved through intervention, it makes becoming aware of the danger signs of suicide all the more important.

Wrobleski believes that the number one danger sign is when a person talks about suicide. She also notes that the most frequent warning signals are those given verbally.

Elaine Gracia, twenty-five, of Las Vegas, who attempted suicide when she was eighteen, had given many of the danger signs. She was in counseling at the time, and in retrospect she says, "I didn't really want to die. I just wanted to end the pain."

"I was in counseling for quite a while before the suicide attempt. I was really messed up. I guess I was looking for somebody to scream out to help me, but it wasn't working. I didn't think anybody understood and it wasn't getting through," says Elaine.

"I was no longer just thinking about it. It was something I wanted to do."

"I don't know where the idea for the suicide came from. It was just there. It just came. It was as strong as the urge to live must be. It seemed just another instinct. I thought about it for so long and finally, I no longer thought about it. I said, 'This is what I'm going to do. I'm not happy. I don't want to live.' You know you're not going to get run over and die, so you just have to go out and do it yourself."

Her stay in the hospital after the attempt changed her thinking. "It shook me. I realized a lot when I was in there. I still had the same feelings. They didn't go away. But I didn't like being locked up in that place. I missed little things — to come and go and to sit outside and talk to friends. I asked myself, 'Do I really want to lose all this?'"

Her counselor was "shook up" about the attempt and told Elaine that she (the counselor) had lost her objectivity. "She told me she was too close to the situation," says Elaine. The two are still friends and Elaine frequents the same counseling center, but sees a different therapist.

Elaine believes this is why parents and close friends can only listen and guide you to professional help when a person begins talking about suicide. "You have to talk to someone who can be objective and not give their opinions of how wrong it would be of you to commit suicide. Statements such as, 'But you have so much to live for,' or 'Why would someone like you want to commit suicide?' have no meaning to the person who is engulfed in suicidal thought."

She was twenty when she went back into counseling. "For a while I just sort of existed—went with the flow. My life didn't get better, and I had to see if I could make it better."

"Things started coming around. My perception changed. I just started enjoying life again. I was still doing drugs, but I was older, out of school and I wasn't suffering from the pressure of school."

Although Elaine was still taking drugs, she was able to look back on the suicide attempt and say, "How could I have done that? Life is a growing process and every day I began to appreciate life a little more. It took time to work through and let things change."

Elaine was finally able to give up drugs, although she says it's a continuing battle, and she occasionally slips back into counseling for the needed support.

"Drugs didn't make me attempt suicide. The life and the past memories that I hadn't dealt with helped cause the suicide attempt."

Elaine is backed up here by health professionals who say that drugs and alcohol don't cause suicide. They simply lower the inhibitions about going ahead with plans to end a life. Using drugs and alcohol is just another way of trying to deal with the pain and hurt of what's going on in a person's life.

"Most people who do drugs do it for a reason. They're trying to cover up something or get a feeling they can't get anywhere else. They don't do drugs just for the heck of it, and they don't do drugs just because the other kids are doing it. Until I got counseling I didn't realize there were more serious reasons. And some of those same reasons led to the suicide attempt. It's not one thing. It's a hundred things that build on you and make you do it.

"You've got to just hang in there and get help. If it takes going to twenty people before you find somebody that makes you comfortable — a qualified professional — then it's worth it," she says.

Elaine believes it's okay to reach out to parents and friends, but that's only a beginning. By the time a person is contemplating suicide, they need professional help. Parents and friends can listen, and then encourage the person to get in touch with a professional.

These parents and friends shouldn't try to be therapists offering advice. "They don't know how to give the right help. Most of your friends aren't going to see that threats of suicide are serious and need to be dealt with in a serious way."

Elaine believes we have to take suicide out of the closet and start talking about it. She doesn't hesitate to flat out ask someone who's showing signs of suicide, "Are you thinking of committing suicide?"

Then she just listens to them and suggests they get the proper help.

"If I hear someone say, 'I wish I was dead,' I don't take that as a light remark. And I don't beat around the bush. I just ask them if they're contemplating suicide. If the person thinks someone cares about their problem, it helps.

"Just listen to them. Tell them you love them and what to do to get help."

Elaine doesn't mind her real name being used because, "I realize somebody has to speak out, and why not me. I care. I care so much, so if it is the one thing I can do to help someone else who's thinking of suicide, I'll do it."

She acknowledges that some people think they don't have the money to pay for counseling. "But the fact is," she says. "There is help for everyone." Most states have programs that assist in counseling fees.

Jan Fawcett, M.D. professor of psychiatry at Rush Medical College in Chicago Illinois, writes in a pamphlet, *Be-*

fore It's Too Late, prepared by the American Association of Suicidology, "The saddest and most common phrase heard by someone who deals with suicide is, 'I didn't think he'd really do it.' Number two is, 'He just wasn't the type.' In case after case, people have seen clear signs of suicidal behavior but have refused to believe that the danger was real and have failed to do anything about it. As a result, many people die whose lives could have been saved.

"When someone talks about wanting to die or says he has thoughts about suicide, don't be afraid to discuss it with him. Don't make moral judgments or act shocked or avoid the subject. Ask specific questions about how he feels and why he would want to end his life.

"Too often, people who talk to someone who is suicidal offer such advice as, 'Think how much better off you are than so many people and be grateful for what you have,' or 'Pull yourself together and keep a stiff upper lip.'

"Such advice, well intentioned though it may be, can actually make the situation worse, deepening the sense of guilt that the person probably already feels and making him feel more worthless and hopeless over not being able to pull himself out of it. You can help best by taking the problem seriously, assuring the person that something can be done for him, encouraging him to accept professional help, being a good friend to talk to when he needs you, and getting advice from an expert. Your friendship and your actions could save a life," writes Fawcett.

T. Wilson, whose first suicide attempt was at sixteen, has this to say about friendship. "I know from experience and talking with a couple of other people who have thought about, or attempted suicide, that having someone who cares enough to listen can help. If they would just say they were willing to listen and sat in closer proximity and touched your arm, you would know they were paying attention — I'm here. Feel me."

She says comments such as, "Aw, come on." "Get off it," "Have you eaten today?" and other comments that make light of depression or suicidal talk are extremely irritating to a suicidal person.

"Better to say something like, 'How strongly do you feel like doing it?' or 'Should we get some help?' or 'Do you just want to talk?'" she says.

Wilson attempted suicide twice when she was sixteen, and says she would have tried a third time, probably successfully, if she could have found the bullets to her grandfather's gun that he kept in the house.

Wilson, who is now twenty-one and attending college, acknowledges that she still occasionally has thoughts of suicide, but has enough support systems to help her through the episodes.

No one knew of her first attempt as a teen when she took, "bottles of pills," and went to bed expecting to die. The pills made her sick, and she threw them up later in the night.

The second attempt, also as a teen, involved slashing her wrists. A friend took her to a doctor who simply treated the wounds and dismissed her without mentioning how she got the cuts. She was living alone at the time and it wasn't until she was eighteen and living with her grandparents that she sought help from a professor who was teaching a class in psychology that she attended.

The professor directed her to a counselor at the school and she began therapy.

"It's been a rough road going through counseling. In our family, we have a rule that you don't talk about your emotions. None of them know to this day what I went through.

"But I've developed my own support group, and I'm involved in a Bible study class where I have some friends. I can say to them, 'Hey, I really feel down. Let's talk or do anything.'

"Some of my friends know about my suicide attempts, but they don't know the circumstances and haven't asked. I've never really said much because it's been so hard. I hate to admit, even now, that I have these thoughts. I'm on medication for depression, and I used to have hangups about taking the medication," she says.

But she says the psychiatrist she now sees is helping her through all that. "He doesn't hold any judgment and that's a big help. A supportive family would be a big help, but I've come to terms with the fact that I will never have that."

Keeping a journal, which Wilson has done since the age of thirteen, has helped. She was an abused child. "If you can't talk about it, at least you can write about it, and it's been a big help. Once I get it out on paper, I start looking at other ways in life that I can handle it."

Here is one of the poems, titled "One Night," that she wrote at age sixteen and entered in her journal.

> I sat on the bed
> waiting for the right moment
>
> Soon.
> Very soon.
> I had made sure everything would be right
> the razor
> silver and sharp
> gleams against the candlelight
> Soon.
> Very soon.
> I won't make a sound
> the razors edge
> gliding on the skin of my wrist
> at last I feel the warmth
> that I've always wanted to feel
> the dark red blood runs down my arm
> and now the next wrist.

the beauty of the blood
seen by the candlelight
is kind of lonely with no one to see my ecstasy
oh well, no big loss.
Soon.
Very soon.
my misery will end
no more
my misery will end

"The poem seems gruesome now. I certainly see that now, but I also see that I needed warmth. A simple hug would have been great. A simple, 'I love you' would have been great, especially at the time I wrote it," she says.

"I keep wondering why I never put a period on the last line of the poem. I don't know if that was a statement in itself, or what."

The best form of prevention is an early awareness that a problem may exist. It is important to be on the alert for any of the following danger signs, even in a casual acquaintance because, like Wilson, some people may not have adequate support from friends or family.

SUICIDE WARNING SIGNS

1. Suicide threats.
2. Previous suicide attempts.
3. Statements revealing a desire to die.
4. A preoccupation with and asking questions about death.
5. Getting affairs in order.
6. Giving personal effects away.
7. Personality changes or odd behavior.
8. Withdrawal, apathy, moodiness, anger, crying, sleeplessness, lack of appetite.
9. Loss of interest in usual activities.
10. Tendency toward isolation.
11. Statements about hopelessness, helplessness or worthlessness.
12. Sudden appearance of happiness and calmness after a period of some of the characteristics listed above.

If you, or a friend or relative show any of the above symptoms, The American Association of Suicidology recommends getting help from the following sources:

Suicide prevention centers.
Crisis intervention centers.
Mental health clinics.
Hospitals.
Family physicians.
The clergy.

Please see the resource guide at the end of this book for detailed listings of where to get help.

8
SURVIVORS
OF
SUICIDE

Writing this book has been an enlightening experience for me. Attitudes that I began with were changed and some of my own beliefs in the mythology of suicide have been dispelled. I feel fortunate to have shared in the lives of others. Like many of the survivors, life has taken on a richer meaning, and that may be because death has become closer and more meaningful to me.

Elisabeth Kübler-Ross has said that only when we are able to accept our own, ultimate death, can we truly experience life to its fullest. It isn't that we don't have to put up a fight for life, but that we need to accept death as a natural part of that life.

The words of the holocaust survivor related in Leslie Elliott's story have become part of my lexicon: "Suffering is normal." But so is living.

The survivors survive and life goes on.

Jean Mathews is involved in cross-country skiing, a choral singing group, works at a job she enjoys, visits her children and grandchildren, travels, takes part in theater activities and cherishes her friends. Her friends look to her as a role model. She's one tough lady.

Carol V. has made peace with her father. She writes about people who have surmounted obstacles and made their lives, and the lives of others, more abundant in the process. Yes, she is still angry about her sister's death, and perhaps, we should never be complacent about suicide. It should trouble us. There is no learning, no growth without confrontation.

Jack Simonson has developed stronger ties with his own sons. He's broken the barrier to acknowledging love simply by saying, "I want you to know I love you."

Leslie Elliott knows of suffering and he understands it in other people. Therefore, they can talk to him and know he listens without casting a stone.

Taffy Hoffman, a nurse, wants not only to help heal physical wounds, but knows emotional hurts can cut just as deeply.

Elaine Gracia is not afraid to speak out about her own suicide attempt. She's a survivor in the strongest sense of the word, and by her actions, she might prevent someone else from taking his or her own life.

Adina Wrobleski, whose stepdaughter took her own life, has dedicated herself to enlightening the community about suicide.

Ira and Jeanne Jacoves, through the Jonathan Jacoves

Memorial, have made it possible for other survivors to come together in mutual support.

Chip Frye volunteers his time to help others step back from the whirlpool of suicidal potential.

Covell Hart is able to share his own suicide attempt with those to whom he ministers with deep compassion and nonjudgmental understanding.

Phyllis Hart combines religion and psychology to foster greater understanding for people in crisis.

Diane C. lends support to other women whose husband's have committed suicide.

T. Wilson encourages people to extend a true hand of friendship.

Those in the mental health community, despite their differences of opinion, are working to make the community more healthful, and to rid itself of the stigma, taboos and myths surrounding suicide. The clergy is struggling with the concept of suicide, but in the meantime, giving comfort to its victims.

Once the suicide occurs, the deed is done and acceptance begins for the family and friends left behind. Whether we're the survivors, or the supporters of the survivors, love and understanding must mingle with the debris of tragedy.

Few escape adversity in life. But the choice of how, when, where and for how long we work out our grief is our own lonely decision.

No one should have to hide their grief with the thought in mind that society sets limits and bounds on it.

Judith Bernstein, a psychotherapist who specializes in bereavement, and who heads the survivors of suicide support group at the University of Judaism in Los Angeles, acknowledges that even though sixteen years have passed since her brother's death by suicide, she still grieves — differently than she did at first, but nonetheless, she still feels the loss.

"My brother's death was definitely the reason I went into this type of work. Many of us who go into this type of work are memorializing their children, siblings or spouses by doing something positive and constructive.

"I'm well past the point of working out my grief, but I'm in a position of helping others because of where I've been."

Many survivors step into new areas of their lives once past the first stages of grief.

Judith's mother changed careers a few years after her son's death. She's now deeply involved as an environmentalist. "She put her energy into some things that are enormously helpful to the world. It pushed her into achieving and doing things for herself — to feel that she could and should make a contribution," says Judith.

"We know that's how many people respond to various kinds of losses, not just suicide. They make these changes in their lives and often it's a healthy adjustment for them."

Their lives become richer in one respect, but the loss of a loved one will always tarnish the gold.

Suicide will not disappear from the face of the earth, and neither will the attending grief. But we can lessen the ignorance surrounding it, and therefore become more sensitive to those who are struggling to continue their lives in the face of adversity.

David Hoffman, whose poem "This Ain't No Nightmare" opened Chapter Two, wrote the following poem one year after his brother's suicide. It is a poignant reminder to all survivors of suicide that a new awareness of life can come out of their devastating loss.

Life's Foundations

A year ago the foundations of my world
    were swept from under my feet.
and I learned it was harsh and cold and bitter
    out there, disorderly, not neat.

I cried and bled and struggled through
    the slop and slime, trying
    to stay atop the crumbling morass
    trying to stop the feeling of falling
    into a never-ending pit.
Trying to maintain the barest handhold
    to the world I had known.

It's been a year.
I faltered and slipped and even fell
    once or twice (or more),
But I was able to pick myself up.
At first, that's all I could do.
Once I conquered that feat,
    I began to rebuild.

The physical foundation was the easy part.
I raised myself from the muck and mire,
    dried off in the summer sun and
    the winter's fire.
My body functioned again.

The emotional foundation was tougher.
    is tougher.
There are still cracks in the facade,
    and the supports underneath are shaky at best.
A stilt-house in the middle of a flood is
    safer, stronger and solider than I.
But I'm up.
And each day, my foundations get stronger.
I have solid footing
    and my mind functions again.
I can withstand all but the fiercest of torrents.

Now, I'm aware of just how fragile our foundations are.
Paradoxically, this knowledge of fragility,
Strengthens me.
It anchors my cornerstone.
It gives me strength — physical, mental and emotional.

My cornerstone and your tombstone.
Now I understand how fragile life is.

SUGGESTED READINGS

Dunne, E.J. (Ed.) *Suicide And Its Aftermath.* New York: W.W. Norton, 1987.

Evans, G. and Farberow, N.L. *The Encyclopedia Of Suicide.* New York: News/Facts On File, 1988.

Ginsburg, G. *To Live Again: Rebuilding Your Life After You've Become A Widow.* Los Angeles: Jeremy P. Tarcher, 1987.

Hendin, H. *Suicide In America.* New York: W.W. Norton, 1982.

Hewett, J.H. *After Suicide.* Philadelphia: Westminster Press, 1980.

Juneau, B. *Sad But O.K., My Daddy Died Today.* Grass Valley, CA: Blue Dolphin Press, 1988.

Klagsbrun, F. *Too Young To Die.* New York: Pocket Books, 1981.

Lukas, C. and Seiden, H. *Silent Grief.* New York: Charles Scribner's Sons, 1987.

Miller, A. *The Enabler: When Helping Harms The Ones You Love.* Claremont, CA: Hunter House, 1988.

Moffatt, B. (Ed.) *AIDS: A Self-Care Manual.* Santa Monica, CA: IBS Press, 1987.

Moffatt, B. *Gifts For The Living: Conversations With Caregivers On Death And Dying.* Santa Monica, CA: IBS Press, 1988.

Moffatt, B. *When Someone You Love Has AIDS.* New York: NAL Penguin, 1986.

Parrish-Harra, C.W. *The New Age Handbook On Death And Dying.* Santa Monica, CA: IBS Press, 1989.

Roth, D. (Ed.) *Stepping Stones To Grief Recovery.* Santa Monica, CA: IBS Press, 1988.

Roy, A. (Ed.) *Suicide.* Baltimore: Williams and Wilkins, 1986.

Shneidman, E. *Definition of Suicide.* New York: John Wiley & Sons, 1986.

Spillard, A. *Grief After Suicide.* Pamphlet available from: WMHA, 414 W. Moreland Blvd., #101, Waukesha, WI 53186.

Stauffer, E. *Unconditional Love And Forgiveness.* Burbank, CA: Triangle Publishers, 1987.

Wrobleski, A.
  Suicide Survivors Grief Group
  Suicide: Questions And Answers
  Suicide: The Danger Signs
  Suicide: Your Child Has Died
  Booklets available from:
  5124 Grove Street
  Minneapolis, MN 55436.

WHERE TO GET HELP

If you, or a friend or relative show any suicidal tendencies, The American Association of Suicidology recommends getting help from the following sources:

Suicide prevention centers.
Crisis intervention centers.
Mental health clinics.
Hospitals.
Family physicians.
The clergy.

For further information on where to get help in your area, contact:

National Institute of Mental Health Public Information
5600 Fishers Lane
Rockville, Maryland 20857
(301) 443-4536.

American Association of Suicidology Central
2459 S. Ash St.
Denver, Colorado 80222
(303) 692-0985.

Individual listings by state for survivors of suicide groups and prevention/crisis centers follow. All hotlines throughout the nation can give referrals for people who are contemplating or who have attempted suicide.

PREVENTION AND CRISIS CENTERS

ALABAMA

CONTACT MOBILE
P.O. BOX 66608
MOBILE, AL 36660
(205)438-4200

CRISIS CENTER
3600 8TH AVE. S., SUITE 501
BIRMINGHAM, AL 35222
(205)323-7782

ALASKA

C.R.I.S.I.S
2611 FAIRBANKS ST.
ANCHORAGE, AK 99503
(902)272-2496

MENTAL HEALTH SERVICES
4020 FOLKER
ANCHORAGE, AK 99508
(907)563-1000

CRISIS LINE
P.O. BOX 873388
WASILLA, AK 99687
(907)376-3356

CRISIS CLINIC
P.O. BOX 832
FAIRBANKS, AK 99707
(907)479-0166

ARIZONA

CHICANOS POR LA CAUSA
1402 S. CENTRAL
PHOENIX, AZ 85003
(602)258-3641

ARKANSAS

CRISIS INTERVENTION
P.O. BOX 1618
SPRINGDALE, AR 72765
(501)756-1995

CALIFORNIA

HELP, INC.
P.O. BOX 2498
REDDING, CA 96099
(916)225-5255

SUICIDE PREVENTION
P.O. BOX 622
DAVIS, CA 95617
(916)756-7542

SUICIDE PREVENTION
P.O. BOX 449
SACRAMENTO, CA 95802
(916)441-1138

SUICIDE PREVENTION
P.O. BOX 2444
NAPA, CA 94558
(707)257-3470

CRISIS-HELP
1360 ADAMS ST.
ST HELENA, CA 94574
(707)942-4319

SUICIDE INTERVENTION
P.O. BOX 4852
WALNUT CREEK, CA 94596
(415)939-1916

SUICIDE PREVENTION
P.O. BOX 9102
BERKELEY, CA 94709
(415)848-1515

SUICIDE PREVENTION
6940 GEARY BLVD.
SAN FRANCISCO, CA 94118
(415)752-4866

SUICIDE PREVENTION
1811 TROUSDALE DR.
BURLINGAME, CA 94010
(415)877-5604

MENTAL HEALTH SERVICES
3800 S. FAIRWAY ST.
VISALIA, CA 93277
(209)732-6631

HELP IN EMOTIONAL
TROUBLE
P.O. BOX 4282
FRESNO, CA 93744
(209)486-4703

SUICIDE PREVENTION
P.O. BOX 734
CAPITOLA, CA 95010
(408)426-2342

SUICIDE PREVENTION
P.O. BOX 52078
PACIFIC GROVE, CA 93950
(408)375-6966

CALL-LINE
P.O. BOX 14567
SANTA BARBARA, CA 93107
(805)961-4114

SUICIDE PREVENTION
1041 S. MENLO
LOS ANGELES, CA 90006
(213)386-5111

HOTLINE HELP CENTER
P.O. BOX 999
ANAHEIM, CA 92805
(714)778-1000

SUICIDE & CRISIS
 INTERVENTION
1669 N. "E" ST.
SAN BERNADINO, CA 92405
(714)886-6730

ARMY COMMUNITY SERVICE
BLDG. 548 ATTN: AFZJ-PAP-A
FORT IRWIN, CA 92310
(619)386-3695

THE CRISIS TEAM
P.O. BOX 85524
SAN DIEGO, CA 92138
(619)236-4576

SUICIDE HOTLINE
120 ELM ST.
SAN DIEGO, CA 92101
(619)232-4331

COLORADO

CRISIS HELPLINE
700 W. MOUNTAIN AVE.
FT. COLLINS, CO 80521
(303)493-3896

SUICIDE AND CRISIS
2459 SOUTH ASH
DENVER, CO 80222
(303)756-8485

SUICIDE PREVENTION
229 COLORADO AVE.
PUEBLO, CO 81004
(303)545-2477

MENTAL HEALTH CENTER
6195 W. 38TH AVE.
WHEAT RIDGE, CO 80033
(303)425-0300

CONNECTICUT

HOTLINE
189 MASON ST.
GREENWICH, CT 06830
(203)661-4378

THE WHEELER CLINIC
91 NORTHWEST DR.
PLAINVILLE, CT 06062
(203)747-6801

DISTRICT OF COLUMBIA

FACT HOTLINE
2001 "O" ST. NW, SUITE G-100
WASHINGTON, DC 20036
(202)965-1900

ST. FRANCIS CENTER
2201 "P" ST. NW
WASHINGTON, DC 20037
(202)234-5613

THE SAMARITANS
4115 WISCONSIN AVE. NW
WASHINGTON, DC 20016
(202)546-1544

FLORIDA

TELEPHONE COUNSEL
P.O. BOX 20169
TALLAHASSEE, FL 32316
(904)224-6333

SUICIDE PREVENTION
2218 PARK ST.
JACKSONVILLE, FL 32204
(904)387-5641

CRISIS CENTER
730 N. WALDO RD. SUITE 100
GAINESVILLE, FL 32601
(904)372-3659

HELPLINE
5900 JUNIOR COLLEGE RD.
KEY WEST, FL 33040
(305)294-5531

MENTAL HEALTH SERVICES
2520 NORTH ORANGE AVE.
ORLANDO, FL 32804
(305)896-9306

SUICIDE PREVENTION
COLLEGE OF EDUCATION
U. OF CENTRAL FLORIDA
ORLANDO, FL 32816
(305)275-2068

SUICIDE/CRISIS HOTLINE
566 BARTON BLVD., #304
ROCKLEDGE, FL 32955
(305)631-9790

SWITCHBOARD OF MIAMI
35 SW 8TH ST.
MIAMI, FL 33130
(305)358-1640

CRISIS LINE
P.O. BOX 22877
FORT LAUDERDALE, FL 33335
(305)524-8371

CRISIS LINE
P.O. BOX 15522
W. PALM BEACH, FL 33416
(305)689-3334

SUICIDE & CRISIS CENTER
2214 E. HENRY AVE.
TAMPA, FL 33610
(813) 238-8411

GEORGIA

EMERGENCY MENTAL
HEALTH SERVICE
99 BUTLER SE
ATLANTA, GA 30311
(404) 522-9222

HAWAII

SUICIDE AND CRISIS CENTER
200 N. VINEYARD BLVD.
RM 603
HONOLULU, HI 96817
(808) 536-7234

ILLINOIS

CALL FOR HELP
500 WILSHIRE DR.
BELLEVILLE, IL 62223
(618) 397-0968

CRISIS SERVICES
P.O. BOX 570
WOOD RIVER, IL 62095
(618) 251-4073

SAMARITANS
5638 S. WOODLAWN AVE.
CHICAGO, IL 60637
(312) 947-8844

CRISIS CENTER
P.O. BOX 1390
ELGIN, IL 60121
(312) 742-4031

CRISIS LINE
309 W. NEW INDIAN TRAIL CT.
AURORA, IL 60506
(312) 897-5531

SPOON RIVER MHC
302 E. MAIN ST., SUITE 530
GALESBURG, IL 61401
(309) 343-5155

EMERGENCY CRISIS
108 W. MARKET
BLOOMINGTON, IL 61701
(309) 827-5351

CONTACT ROCKFORD
P.O. BOX 1976
ROCKFORD, IL 61110
(815) 964-0400

INDIANA

CRISIS & SUICIDE SERVICE
1433 N. MERIDAN ST., RM 202
INDIANAPOLIS, IN 46202
(317) 269-1569

MENTAL HEALTH CENTER
415 MULBERRY
EVANSVILLE, IN 47713
(812) 423-7791

IOWA

FOUNDATION 2
1251 THIRD AVE. SE
CEDAR RAPIDS, IA 52403
(319) 362-2176

KANSAS

DEPT. OF MENTAL HEALTH
1801 E. TENTH ST.
WICHITA, KS 67214
(316) 268-8251

KENTUCKY

SUICIDE PREVENTION
982 EASTERN PKWY
LOUISVILLE, KY 40217
(502)635-5924

CRISIS CENTER
600 S. PRESTON ST.
LOUISVILLE, KY 40202
(502)924-1595

EMERGENCY SERVICES
324 CUNDIFF SQ.
SOMERSET, KY 42501
(606)679-7348

LOUISIANA

HELP LINE
P.O. BOX 815
DE RIDDER, LA 70634
(318)462-1452

CRISIS PHONE (439-CARE)
1146 HODGES
LAKE CHARLES, LA 70601
(318)433-1062

CRISIS LINE
2515 CANAL ST., SUITE 200
NEW ORLEANS, LA 70119
(504)821-1024

JEWISH FAMILY SERVICES
2026 ST. CHARLES AVE.
NEW ORLEANS, LA 70130
(504)524-8475

CRISIS CENTER
2424 BUNKER HILL DR., #1000
BATON ROUGE, LA 70808
(504)924-1595

CRISIS CENTER
1525 RIVER OAKS RD. W.
NEW ORLEANS, LA 70123
(504)734-1740

MAINE

CRISIS STABILIZATION UNIT
147 WATER ST.
SKOWHEGAN, ME 04976
(207)474-2506

MARYLAND

YOUTH SERVICES
8303 LIBERTY RD.
BALTIMORE, MD 21207
(301)521-4141

COUNTY HOTLINE
6607 RIVERDALE RD.
RIVERDALE, MD 20737
(301)577-3140

COUNTY HOTLINE
10920 CONNECTICUT AVE.
KENSINGTON, MD 20795
(301)949-1255

MASSACHUSSETTS

SAMARITANS
386 STANLEY ST.
FALL RIVER, MA 02720
(617)636-6111

SAMARITANS
73 UNION AVE.
FRAMINGHAM, MA 01701
(617)875-4500

SAMARITANS
55 JACKSON ST.
LAWRENCE, MA 01840
(617) 688-6607

TRI-LINK
51 EVERETT ST.
SOUTHBRIDGE, MA 01550
(617) 765-9101

SAMARITANS
500 COMMONWEALTH AVE.
BOSTON, MA 02215
(617) 536-2460

SAMARITANS
P.O. BOX 65
FALMOUTH, MA 02540
(617) 548-8900

MENTAL HEALTH CENTER
351 ESSEX ST.
LAWRENCE, MA 01840
(617) 683-6303

EMERGENCY TEAM
91 CENTRAL ST.
NORWOOD, MA 02062
(617) 769-6060

CRISIS CENTER
P.O. BOX 652
WORCESTER, MA 01602
(617) 791-7205

MICHIGAN

MENTAL HEALTH
P.O. BOX 127
HART, MI 49420
(616) 873-2108

MENTAL HEALTH SERVICES
125 E. SOUTHERN
MUSKEGON, MI 49442
(616) 726-5266

GRYPHON PLACE
1104 S. WESTNEDGE
KALAMAZOO, MI 49008
(616) 381-1510

SUICIDE PREVENTION
220 BAGLEY, SUITE 626
DETROIT, MI 48226
(313) 963-7890

MENTAL HEALTH CENTER
1575 SUNCREST DR.
LAPEER, MI 48446
(313) 667-0500

CTR. FOR HUMAN RESOURCES
1113 MILITARY ST.
PORT HURON, MI 48060
(313) 985-5168

CRISIS CENTER
5TH FLR, COUNTY BLDG.
MT CLEMENS, MI 48043
(313) 573-8700

MENTAL HEALTH CLINIC
1501 KRAFFT RD.
PORT HURON, MI 48060
(313) 985-5125

MENTAL HEALTH SERVICES
3415 28TH ST.
PORT HURON, MI 48060
(313) 985-9618

MINNESOTA

SUICIDE HELP CENTER
P.O. BOX 34
ROCHESTER, MN 55903
(507) 282-2723

24 HOUR CRISIS HOTLINE
1224 FOURTH AVE.
WORTHINGTON, MN 56187
(507) 372-7671

CRISIS CENTER
701 PARK AVE. SOUTH
MINNEAPOLIS, MN 55415
(612) 347-3164

MISSISSIPPI

GOLDEN TRIANGLE
P.O. BOX 1304
COLUMBUS, MS 39703
(601) 328-0200

MISSOURI

LIFE CRISIS SERVICES
1423 S. BIG BEND BLVD.
ST LOUIS, MO 63117
(314) 647-3100

NEVADA

CRISIS CENTER
P.O. BOX 8016
RENO, NV 89507
(702) 323-4533

NEW HAMPSHIRE

CRISIS UNIT
18 BAILEY AVE.
CLAREMONT, NH 03743
(603) 542-2578

GUIDANCE CENTER
130 CENTRAL AVE.
DOVER, NH 03820
(603) 742-0630

MENTAL HEALTH CENTER
401 CYPRESS ST.
MANCHESTER, NH 03103
(603) 668-4111

CENTER FOR LIFE
44 STILES RD
SALEM, NH 03079
(603) 893-3548

EMERGENCY SERVICES
P.O. BOX 2032
CONCORD, NH 03301
(603) 228-1551

HEADREST INC
P.O. BOX 221
LEBANON, NH 03766
(603) 448-4872

MENTAL HEALTH CENTER
1145 SAGAMORE AVE.
PORTSMOUTH, NH 03801
(603) 431-6703

NEW JERSEY

MENTAL HEALTH CENTER
646B VALLEY BROOK AVE.
LYNDHURST, NJ 07071
(201) 460-3510

NEW YORK

CRISIS COUNSELING
2740 MARTIN AVE.
BELLMORE, NY 11710
(516)826-0244

RESPONSE
P.O. BOX 300
STONYBROOK, NY 11790
(516)751-7620

LIFE LINE
973 EAST AVE.
ROCHESTER, NY 14607
(716)271-3540

SUICIDE PREVENTION
P.O. BOX 312
ITHACA, NY 14850
(607)272-1505

NORTH CAROLINA

SUICIDE & CRISIS
P.O. BOX 2573
BURLINGTON, NC 27215
(919)228-1720

HELPLINE
414 E. MAIN ST.
DURHAM, NC 27701
(919)683-2392

TO LIFE
P.O. BOX 9354
CHARLOTTE, NC 28299
(704)332-LIFE

NORTH DAKOTA

WOMEN'S RESOURCE
HIGHWAY99 NW
BEULAH, ND 58523
(701)873-2274

OHIO

CRISIS CENTER
2421 13TH ST. NW
CANTON, OH 44708
(216)452-9812

SUPPORT
1361 W. MARKET ST.
AKRON, OH 44313
(216)864-7743

CONTACT
P.O. BOX 1403
WARREN, OH 44482
(216)395-5255

HELP HOTLINE
P.O. BOX 46
YOUNGSTOWN, OH 44501
(216)747-5111

281-CARE
3891 READING RD.
CINCINNATI, OH 45206
(513)281-2866

SUICIDE PREVENTION
184 SALEM AVE.
DAYTON, OH 45406
(513)223-9096

HOPE LINE
P.O. BOX 142
MT. GILEAD, OH 43338
(419)947-2520

RESCUE CRISIS SERVICE
3314 COLLINGWOOD AVE.
TOLEDO, OH 43610
(419) 255-5500

CRISIS HOTLINE
2845 BELL ST.
ZANESVILLE, OH 43701
(614) 454-9766

SUICIDE PREVENTION
1301 HIGH
COLUMBUS, OH 43201
(614) 299-6600

HELP ANONYMOUS
11 E. CENTRAL AVE.
DELAWARE, OH 43015
(614) 363-1835

OKLAHOMA

CONTACT
P.O. BOX 12832
OKLAHOMA CITY, OK 73157
(405) 840-9396

OREGON

CRISIS SERVICE
P.O. BOX 637
PORTLAND, OR 97207
(503) 226-3099

PENNSYLVANIA

CONTACT
P.O. BOX 111294
PITTSBURGH, PA 15238
(412) 963-6416

HELPLINE
200 ROSS ST.
PITTSBURGH, PA 15219
(412) 255-1133

CRISIS CENTER
FITZGERALD
MERCY HOSPITAL
DARBY, PA 19023
(215) 565-2041

RHODE ISLAND

SAMARITANS
33 CHESTNUT ST.
PROVIDENCE, RI 02903
(401) 272-4044

SOUTH CAROLINA

HELP LINE
P.O. BOX 2712
AIKEN, SC 29801
(803) 648-0000

HELPLINE
P.O. BOX 6336
COLUMBIA, SC 29260
(803) 799-6329

TENNESSEE

SUICIDE/CRISIS
P.O. BOX 40068
MEMPHIS, TN 38104
(901) 276-1111

CRISIS CENTER
P.O. BOX 120934
NASHVILLE, TN 37212
(615) 298-3359

TEXAS

SUICIDE PREVENTION
P.O. BOX 3250
AMARILLO, TX 79106
(806)353-7235

CRISIS SERVICES
4906-B EVERHART
CORPUS CHRISTI, TX 78411
(512)993-7416

HELP LINE
P.O. BOX 898
SAN ANTONIO, TX 78293
(512)224-5000

CONTACT
P.O. BOX 742224
DALLAS, TX 75374
(214)233-0866

SUICIDE & CRISIS
2808 SWISS AVE.
DALLAS, TX 75204
(214)824-7020

SAMARITANS
P.O. BOX 50029
DALLAS, TX 75250
(214)243-6110

CRISIS
716 MAGNOLIA
FT. WORTH, TX 76104
(817)336-0108

CRISIS
P.O. BOX 13066
HOUSTON, TX 77219
(713)527-9426

RX FOR CRISIS
P.O. BOX 272651
HOUSTON, TX 77277
(713)795-4511

CENTER FOR ADVANCE
244 N. MAGDALEN
SAN ANGELO, TX 76903
(915)655-8965

SUICIDE CRISIS
P.O. BOX 5011
BEAUMONT, TX 77706
(409)832-6530

UTAH

CRISIS LINE
P.O. BOX 1375
PROVO, UT 84603
(801)377-8255

VIRGINIA

SUICIDE-CRISIS CENTER
P.O. BOX 1493
PORTSMOUTN, VA 23705
(804)393-0502

HOTLINE
P.O. BOX 187
ARLINGTON, VA 22210
(703)522-4460

WASHINGTON

CARE CRISIS LINE
2801 LOMBARD AVE.
EVERETT, WA 98201
(206)259-3191

MENTAL HEALTH
9108 LAKEWOOD DR.
TACOMA, WA 98499
(206)584-8933

CRISIS CLINIC
1530 EASTLAKE E.
SEATTLE, WA 98102
(206)447-3210

YOUTH SUICIDE
22226 4TH PL. W.
BOTHELL, WA 98021
(206)481-0560

WISCONSIN

SUICIDE PREVENTION
1221 WHIPPLE ST.
EAU CLAIRE, WI 54701
(715)839-3274

MENTAL HEALTH CENTER
31 S. HENRY
MADISON, WI 53703
(608)251-2341

MENTAL HEALTH SERVICE
8700 W. WISCONSIN AVE.
MILWAUKEE, WI 53226
(414)257-7222

COUNSELING
P.O. BOX 1005
ELKHORN, WI 53121
(414)741-3200

HELPLINE
P.O. BOX 1141
OSHKOSH, WI 54902
(414)233-7709

LIFE LINE
P.O. BOX 2474
APPLETON, WI 54913
(413)734-1434

WYOMING

SUICIDE PREVENTION
611 THELM DR.
CASPER, WY 82609
(307)234-5061

SURVIVORS GROUPS

ALABAMA

ROBERT GODWIN
SURVIVORS OF SUICIDE
260 JACKSON DR.
MOBILE, AL 36609
(205)342-0616

TRINA HICKS
MENTAL HEALTH ASSOC.
3600 8TH AVE. SOUTH
SUITE E111
BIRMINGHAM, AL 35222
(205)322-0445

ALASKA

MARLENE LESLIE
SURVIVORS OF SUICIDE
2611 FAIRBANKS ST., SUITE A
ANCHORAGE, AK 99503
(907)272-2496

FAIRBANKS CRISIS CLINIC
FOUNDATION
P.O. BOX 81804
FAIRBANKS, AK 99708
(907)479-0166

ARIZONA

ILENE DODE
SURVIVORS OF SUICIDE
GROUPS
2024 E. UNIVERSITY
MESA, AZ 85203
(602)844-7320

ILENE DODE
SURVIVORS OF SUICIDE
GROUPS
7835 E. REDFIELD RD.,
SUITE 106
SCOTTSDALE, AZ 85260
(602)948-1860

VICKY STROMEE
SURVIVORS OF SUICIDE
P.O. BOX 43696
TUCSON, AZ 85733
(602)323-9373

CALIFORNIA

HELP INC.
P.O. BOX 2498
REDDING, CA 96099
(916)225-5255

MARILYN KOENIG
FRIENDS FOR SURVIVAL
5701 LERNER WAY
SACRAMENTO, CA 95823
(916)392-0664

GARY MCCONAHAY
SPRING GROUP/FALL GROUP
P.O. BOX 622
DAVIS, CA 95617
(916)756-7542

JANICE CHARLUP
SUICIDE PREVENTION
P.O. BOX 2444
NAPA, CA 94558
(707)554-2510

DIANA DE REGNIER
SUICIDE LOSS SUPPORT
GROUP
P.O. BOX T
NOVATO, CA 94948
(415)892-9235

SUSAN BREED
SURVIVORS OF SUICIDE
P.O. BOX 4852
WALNUT CREEK, CA 94596
(415)944-0645

SUICIDE GRIEF COUNSELING
P.O. BOX 9102
BERKELEY, CA 94541
(415)848-1515

DONNA MORRISH
GRIEF COUNSELING
21636 REDWOOD RD.
CASTRO VALLEY, CA 94546
(415)889-1104

BEA SWANSON
SUICIDE PREVENTION &
CRISIS CENTER
1811 TROUSDALE DR
BURLINGAME, CA 94010
(415)877-5604

JOAN SHELDON
GRIEF COUNSELING
P.O. BOX 792
SAN ANSELMO, CA 94960
(415)454-4544

PATRICK ARBORE
SELF-HELP GRIEF GROUP
3940 GEARY BLVD
SAN FRANCISCO, CA 94118
(415) 752-4866

MEG PARIS
SUICIDE SUPPORT GROUP
2220 MOOR PARK AVE
SAN JOSE, CA 95128
(408) 299-6250

VIRGINIA STEPHENS
SURVIVORS OF SUICIDE
P.O. BOX 52078
PACIFIC GROVE, CA 93950
(408) 375-6966

DICK & SANDY GALLAGHER
SURVIVORS OF SUICIDE
1092 E. SIERRA
FRESNO, CA 93710
(209) 431-8994

HELP IN EMOTIONAL
TROUBLE
P.O. BOX 4282
FRESNO, CA 93744
(209) 486-4703

SUICIDE PREVENTION
1041 S. MENLO AVE.
LOS ANGELES, CA 90006
(213) 386-5111

LAUREL FADKE
SURVIVORS OF SUICIDE
3235 FOURTH AVE
SAN DIEGO, CA 92103
(619) 482-0297

COLORADO

DR. CHERYL CLEMENT
HEARTBEAT
710 33RD ST.
BOULDER, CO 80303
(303) 444-3496

DICK BERGER
SURVIVORS OF SUICIDE
1231 LAFAYETTE
DENVER, CO 80218
(303) 860-7274

NORICE WHEAT
HEARTBEAT
2422 S. DOWNING
DENVER, CO 80210
(303) 777-9234

TALLIE MILLER
SEASONS
589 29 1/2 RD.
GRAND JUNCTION, CO 81504
(303) 245-6039

HEARTBEAT
801 N. SANTA FE AVE.
PUEBLO, CO 81003
(303) 545-2477

LA RITA ARCHIBALD
HEARTBEAT
2015 DEVON
COLORADO SPRINGS, CO
80909
(719) 596-2575

CONNECTICUT

PROF. CLAYTON HEWITT
SURVIVORS OF SUICIDE
MIDDLESEX COMM. COLLEGE
MIDDLETOWN, CT 06457
(203) 344-3043

JOANN MECCA
SUICIDE BEREAVEMENT
P.O. BOX 9185
WETHERSFIELD, CT 06109
(203) 563-3035

THE WHEELER CLINIC
91 NORTHWEST DRIVE
PLAINVILLE, CT 06062
(203) 747-6801

DISTRICT OF COLUMBIA

HISPANIC MHC
1823 18TH ST. NW
WASHINGTON, DC 20009
(202) 387-8926

ST. FRANCIS CENTER
5417 SHERIER PL. NW
WASHINGTON, DC 20016
(202) 363-8500

FLORIDA

EMERGENCY MENTAL
HEALTH SERVICE
11254 58TH ST. N.
PINELLAS PARK, FL 34666-2606
(813) 545-5636

ANITA & KURT HOSIER
LIVING AFTERWARDS
3802 33RD AVE. W.
BRADENTON, FL 34205
(813) 753-1247

DR. DOROTHEA HOVER
SURVIVORS OF SUICIDE
13902 N. FLORIDA AVE
TAMPA, FL 33613
(813) 963-3035

LIFE CENTER
214 S. FIELDING
TAMPA, FL 33606
(813) 251-0289

JEANNE VALIS
CRISIS LINE
1300 S. ANDREWS AVE.
P.O. BOX 22877
FORT LAUDERDALE, FL 33335
(305) 467-6333

ELAINE DELLON
PARENTS OF SUICIDE
9712 SW 131 ST.
MIAMI, FL 33176
(305) 235-4875

JOY RICHTER
SURVIVORS OF SUICIDE
825 W. CENTER ST. 35B
JUPITER, FL 33458
(305) 747-3165

MARGE GREENBAUM
SURVIVORS OF SUICIDE
112 PASADENA PL.
ORLANDO, FL 32803
(305) 425-2624

CRISIS SERVICE
P.O. BOX 1108
ROCKLEDGE, FL 32955
(305) 631-9290

JAMES FORTENBERRY
SURVIVORS OF SUICIDE
2218 PARK ST.
JACKSONVILLE, FL 32204
(904) 387-5641

GEORGIA

BETTY MIKSAD
SUICIDE SURVIVORS
P.O. BOX 1828
ALBANY, GA 31703
(912) 888-4047

SURVIVORS OF SUICIDE
218 HILDERBRAND AVE.
ATLANTA, GA 30328
(404) 256-9797

IDAHO

JOANNE GLENN/JANE SAILOR
SURVIVORS OF SUICIDE
P.O. BOX 8357
BOISE, ID 83707
(208) 362-2858 JOANNE
(208) 385-1850 JANE

ILLINOIS

STEPHANIE WEBER-SLEPICKA
SURVIVORS OF SUICIDE
206 S. FORDHAM
AURORA, IL 60506
(312) 897-5531

JANET MIGDOW
OPTIONS
2320 W. LAWRENCE, SUITE 217
CHICAGO, IL 60625
(312) 989-6856

REV. CHARLES RUBEY
L.O.S.S.
126 N. DESPLAINES ST.
CHICAGO, IL 60606
(312) 876-2260

MARCIE EHRET
SURVIVORS OF SUICIDE
9400 LEBANON RD.
EDGEMONT, IL 62203
(618) 397-0963

INDIANA

VIOLA SEDLACEK
WE THE LIVING
9347 MARYDALE LN.
FORT WAYNE, IN 46804
(219) 432-6293

SHAR JOYCE
SURVIVORS OF SUICIDE
706 SOUTH IRONWOOD
SOUTH BEND, IN 46615
(219) 287-0363

DEE ENRICO-JANIK
MENTAL HEALTH
2450 169TH AVE.
HAMMOND, IN 46323
(219) 845-2720

IOWA

JEFF WHITTLESEY
SURVIVORS OF SUICIDE
1251 THIRD AVE. SE
CEDAR RAPIDS, IA 52403
(319) 362-2174

E. ROSS
P.O. BOX 2323
IOWA CITY, IA 52244
(319) 337-9890

KEITH STOKES
SUICIDE GRIEF SUPPORT
828 WEST FOURTH ST
WATERLOO, IA 50702
(319) 233-5538

E. ROSS
RAY OF HOPE
P.O. BOX 746
COUNCIL BLUFFS, IA 51502
(712) 325-9430

KANSAS

NANCY SEMLER
HEARTBEAT
RR 1
BIRD CITY, KS 67731
(913) 734-2626

KAY OLSON
SURVIVORS OF SUICIDE
1205 HARRISON
TOPEKA, KS 66612
(913) 357-5119

ANN GORRELL
RAY OF HOPE
P.O. BOX 1151
PARSONS, KS 67357
(316) 421-3254

KENTUCKY

JONNIE VATTER
SURVIVORS OF SUICIDE
P.O. BOX 7347
LOUISVILLE, KY 40207
(502) 895-9122

LOUISIANA

CRISIS CENTER
2424 BUNKER HILL DR., #1000
BATON ROUGE, LA 70808
(504) 928-6482

JIM & BARBARA MOORE
SUPPORT AFTER SUICIDE
3804 GOUVILLE DR
MONROE, LA 71201
(318) 323-9479

ROMA MONLEZUN
COPING WITH SUICIDE
8200 HAMPSON, SUITE 300
NEW ORLEANS, LA 70118
(504) 866-1901

MAINE

EMILY GAMACHE
NEW HOPE
P.O. BOX 779
BIDDEFORD, ME 04005
(207) 284-4362

MARYLAND

MARILYN MOSSMAN
SUICIDE BEREAVEMENT
2331 OLD COURT RD.,
SUITE 107
BALTIMORE, MD 21208
(301) 321-4539

CATHERINE BOWIE
SURVIVORS OF SUICIDE
11 COUNTY OAK RD.
MECHANICSVILLE, MD 20659
(301) 884-5503

CORYNE MELTON
SUICIDE BEREAVEMENT
13907 VISTA DR.
ROCKVILLE, MD 20853
(301) 460-4677

DOUGLAS TIPPERMAN
SUICIDE BEREAVEMENT
6805 FAIRFAX RD., APT. 123
BETHESDA, MD 20814
(301)951-3665

SUICIDE HOTLINE
6607 RIVERDALE RD.
RIVERDALE, MD 20737
(301)577-3140

MASSACHUSSETTS

EILEEN WHITE
SAMARITANS
73 UNION AVE.
FRAMINGHAM, MA 01701
(617)875-4500

MARGARET SERLEY
SAMARITANS
55 JACKSON ST
LAWRENCE, MA 01840
(617)688-6607

MICHIGAN

JAY CALLAHAN
SURVIVORS OF SUICIDE
501 N. MAPLE
ANN ARBOR, MI 48103
(313)663-3042

THOSE TOUCHED BY SUICIDE
2200 DUNSTABLE
BIRMINGHAM, MI 48008
(313)646-5224

MARY LEONHARDI
SURVIVORS OF SUICIDE
200 BAGLEY, SUITE 626
DETROIT, MI 48226
(313)224-7000

KAY JOHNSON
CATHOLIC SOCIAL SERVICES
202 E. BOULEVARD LN.,
RM. 210
FLINT, MI 48503
(313)232-9950

MENTAL HEALTH SERVICES
3415 28TH ST.
PORT HURON, MI 48060
(313)985-9618

JACK BURKHARDT
SURVIVORS OF SUICIDE
1401 WHITTIER RD.
GROSSE POINTE PK, MI 48230
(313)882-6508

CENTER FOR HUMAN RE-
SOURCES
1001 MILITARY ST., SUITE 2
PORT HURON, MI 48060
(313)985-5168

SURVIVORS OF SUICIDE
21201 13 MILE RD.
ST. CLAIR SHORE, MI 48082
(313)293-2240

DEBBIE CARLSON
SURVIVORS OF SUICIDE
520 LAKE WINYAH
ALPENA, MI 49707
(517)354-2781

CONRAD SMITH
SURVIVORS OF SUICIDE
142 E. MAUMEE ST., SUITE 107
ADRIAN, MI 49221
(517)263-5810

BARBARA FRENCH
SURVIVORS OF SUICIDE
9250 LOOKING GLASS BROOK
GRAND LEDGE, MI 48837
(517) 626-6317

MABEL LAKE
SURVIVORS OF SUICIDE
745 RIVERSIDE DR.
BATTLE CREEK, MI 49015
(616) 965-5218

MELISSA SJOGRAN
SURVIVORS OF SUICIDE
401 LAKE
CADILLAC, MI 49601
(616) 775-3463

CHERYL ALLEN-HICKS
SURVIVORS OF SUICIDE
23851 MAY ST.
EDWARDSBURG, MI 49112
(616) 699-7472

ETHEL BUCEK
SURVIVORS OF SUICIDE
1777 PINEKNOLL SE
GRAND RAPIDS, MI 49508
(616) 455-0372

GRYPHON PLACE
1104 S. WESTNEDGE
KALAMAZOO, MI 49008
(616) 381-1510

CRISIS CENTER
P.O. BOX 1035
TRAVERSE CITY, MI 49685
(616) 922-4802

MINNESOTA

BEN WOLFE
SURVIVORS OF SUICIDE
407 E. THIRD ST.
DULUTH, MN 55812
(218) 726-4402

VERLYN SMITH
SURVIVORS OF SUICIDE
HARVARD & DELAWARE ST. SE
MINNEAPOLIS, MN 55414
(612) 379-1363

TOM & PAT FLAK
SURVIVORS OF SUICIDE
1400 40TH AVE. NE
MINNEAPOLIS, MN 55421
(612) 788-5811

DENNIS SCHARPEN
SURVIVORS OF SUICIDE
8424 50TH AVE. N.
MINNEAPOLIS, MN 55428
(612) 535-6351

RALPH RICKGARN
412 22 AVENUE SOUTH
MINNEAPOLIS, MN 55455-0424
(612) 625-4570

ROBERTA GOODRICH
SURVIVORS OF SUICIDE
28125 WOODSIDE RD
SHOREWOOD, MN 55331
(612) 474-2472

TONY DEL PERCIO
SURVIVORS OF SUICIDE
1485 WHITE BEAR AVE
ST. PAUL, MN 55106
(612) 776-1565

MISSOURI

SUAN RICHARDSON
RAY OF HOPE
1230 NORTH DUQUESNE
JOPLIN, MO 64801
(417) 358-1373

JANICE NEWHART
SURVIVORS OF SUICIDE
1318 N. CONCORD
SPRINGFIELD, MO 65802
(417) 865-5943

NANCY THURMAN
SURVIVORS OF SUICIDE
1423 S. BIG BEND BLVD.
ST. LOUIS, MO 63117
(314) 647-3100

NEVADA

SUICIDE CRISIS CENTER
P.O. BOX 8016
RENO, NV 89507
(702) 323-6111

NEW HAMPSHIRE

TONI PAUL
COUNSELING ASSOC.
25 S. RIVER RD.
BEDFORD, NH 03102
(603) 623-1916

NANCY CHURCHILL
MENTAL HEALTH SERVICES
P.O. BOX 2032
CONCORD, NH 03301
(603) 228-1551

SAMARITANS
25 LAMSON ST.
KEENE, NH 03431
(603) 357-5505

MENTAL HEALTH CENTER
401 CYPRESS ST.
MANCHESTER, NH 03103
(603) 668-4111

MARIA LEVANDOWSKI
SURVIVORS OF SUICIDE
2013 ELM ST.
MANCHESTER, NH 03104
(603) 644-2525

NEW JERSEY

MENTAL HEALTH CENTER
516 VALLEY BROOK AVE.
LYNDHURST, NJ 07071
(201) 460-3510

KAREN DUNNE-MAXIM
SURVIVORS OF SUICIDE
671 HOES LN.
PISCATAWAY, NJ 08854
(201) 463-4109

NEW MEXICO

CATHERINE EDGAR
GRIEF INTERVENTION
SCHOOL OF MEDICINE
UNIVERSITY OF NEW MEXICO
ALBUQUERQUE, NM 87131
(505) 277-5610

NEW YORK

JULIE BARRETT
SAMARITANS
200 CENTRAL AVE.
ALBANY, NY 12206
(518) 463-0861

DEIRDRE SILVERMAN
AFTER SUICIDE
P.O. BOX 312
ITHACA, NY 14850
(607) 272-1505

BECKY BECKER
AFTER SUICIDE
34 ALFORD ST.
ROCHESTER, NY 14609
(716) 654-7262

CHRISTINE BEATTIE
HOPE FOR SURVIVORS
1342 LANCASTER AVE.
SYRACUSE, NY 13210
(315) 472-4673

C. GIANGRECO
FRIENDS AND RELATIVES
27 SCHERMERHORN ST.
BROOKLYN, NY 11201
(718) 643-1946

THE SAMARITANS
P.O. BOX 1259
NEW YORK, NY 10159
(212) 673-3000

JUDY WOODWARD
SURVIVORS
6241 MT. AIRY RD.
SAUGERTIES, NY 12477
(914) 336-4747

NORTH CAROLINA

TO LIFE
P.O. BOX 9354
CHARLOTTE, NC 28299
(704) 332-LIFE

MONA FREEPERSON
HOPELINE
P.O. BOX 6036
RALEIGH, NC 27628
(919) 755-6588

NORTH DAKOTA

TERRY BARRETT
SUICIDE BEREAVEMENT
3306 2ND ST. NORTH
FARGO, ND 58102
(701) 232-0424

OHIO

ANDREA DENTON
SURVIVORS
513 W. MARKET ST.
AKRON, OH 44303
(216) 434-1214

BETH CRAIG
SURVIVORS
3929 ROCKY RIVER DR.
CLEVELAND, OH 44111
(216) 252-5800

RITA KERR
SURVIVORS OF SUICIDE
1560 FISHINGER RD.
COLUMBUS, OH 43221
(614) 457-7876

HELP ANONYMOUS
11 E. CENTRAL AVE.
DELAWARE, OH 43015
(614) 363-1835

JO ANN SOUDERS
SURVIVORS AFTER SUICIDE
124 ST. LOUIS DR.
OWENSVILLE, OH 45160
(513) 732-1697

BETTY MCDANIEL OETTING
4621 STORMS CREEK RD.
URBANA, OH 43078
(513) 788-2575

CATHY GRIZINSKI
SURVIVORS OF SUICIDE
P.O. BOX 46
YOUNGSTOWN, OH 44501
(216) 758-7983

SUSAN POPOVICI
SURVIVORS
2421 THIRTEENTH ST. NW
CANTON, OH 44708
(216) 452-6000

CAROL STEWART
SURVIVORS OF SUICIDE
360 S. THIRD ST., SUITE 102
COLUMBUS, OH 43215
(614) 464-2646

SURVIVORS OF SUICIDE
P.O. BOX 1393
DAYTON, OH 45401
(513) 223-9096

JUDY FRIDLEY
HOPELINE
P.O. BOX 142
MOUNT GILEAD, OH 43328
(419) 947-2520

LINDA DEASON
SURVIVORS OF SUICIDE
1345 FOUNTAIN BLVD.
SPRINGFIELD, OH 45504
(513) 399-9500, EXT. 287

SURVIVORS OF SUICIDE
924 EASTWIND DR.
WESTERVILLE, OH 43081
(614) 882-9338

OKLAHOMA

CRISIS TELEPHONE
P.O. BOX 26901
OKLAHOMA CITY, OK 73190
(405) 271-3539

PENNSYLVANIA

CONTACT HARRISBURG
P.O. BOX 2328
HARRISBURG, PA 17105
(717) 652-4987

DAVID ZIV
SURVIVORS OF SUICIDE
641 LAWLER ST.
PHILADELPHIA, PA 19116
(215) 969-1436

BONNIE FRANK CARTER
ALBERT EINSTEIN MED. CTR.
DEPT OF PSYCHIATRY
YORK & TABOR RD.
PHILADELPHIA, PA 19141
(215) 456-7240

GRACE MORITZ
SURVIVORS OF SUICIDE
ONE MONROEVILLE CENTER
MONROEVILLE, PA 15146
(412) 624-1442

SUNNIE FREEMAN
SURVIVORS OF SUICIDE
1724 RODMAN ST.
PHILADELPHIA, PA 19146
(215) 545-2242

GRACE MORITZ
SURVIVORS OF SUICIDE
3811 O'HARA ST.
PITTSBURGH, PA 15213
(412) 624-1442

FELICE MASSEY
SURVIVORS SUPPORT
1110 NW END BLVD., RT. 309
QUAKERTOWN, PA 18951
(215)538-2686

RHODE ISLAND

EUNICE BISHOP
SAMARITANS
33 CHESTNUT ST.
PROVIDENCE, RI 02903
(401)272-4243

SOUTH CAROLINA

RANDY ARMSTRONG
SURVIVORS OF SUICIDE
5 MCSWAIN DR.
GREENVILLE, SC 29615
(803)244-6478

SOUTH DAKOTA

MARY JONES
SUICIDE SUPPORT GROUP
304 S. PHILLIPS
SIOUX FALLS, SD 57102
(605)336-1974

TENNESSEE

MARY SEWELL
SURVIVORS OF SUICIDE
P.O. BOX 40068
MEMPHIS, TN 38104
(901)274-7477

CHARTER LAKESIDE
HOSPITAL
2911 BRUNSWICK RD.
MEMPHIS, TN 38134
(901)377-4700

LYDIA WALDROP
SURVIVORS OF SUICIDE
P.O. BOX 7
SOUTH FULTON, TN 38257
(901)479-2688

JEAN ROWLETT
SURVIVORS OF SUICIDE
P.O. BOX 40752
NASHVILLE, TN 37204
(615)244-7444

TEXAS

ESTHER QUINE
SURVIVORS GROUP
P.O. BOX 3250
AMARILLO, TX 79116
(806)353-7235

ROBERT WELLS
SURVIVORS OF SUICIDE
P.O. BOX 6477
LUBBOCK, TX 79493
(806)765-7272

MENTAL HEALTH CENTER
2006 GASTON PL.
AUSTIN, TX 78723
(512)926-7080

DOT BARNETTE
SURVIVORS AFTER SUICIDE
4906-B EVERHART
CORPUS CHRISTI, TX 78411
(512)993-7410

MARY ARCHER
SURVIVORS OF SUICIDE
P.O. BOX 10614
FT. WORTH, TX 76114
(817) 924-9201

SHERYL WHITE
SUICIDE & CRISIS CENTER
2808 SWISS AVE.
DALLAS, TX 75204
(214) 828-1000

BARBARA BLANTON
SURVIVORS OF SUICIDE
P.O. BOX 1808
PLANO, TX 75074
(214) 881-0088

CATHY GRISSOM
CRISIS INTERVENTION
P.O. BOX 130866
HOUSTON, TX 77219
(713) 527-9864

UTAH

CRISIS LINE
P.O. BOX 1375
PROVO, UT 84603
(801) 377-8259

CHRISTINA LARSEN
P.O. BOX 187
PARK CITY, UT 84060
(801) 649-8327

VERMONT

DANNY COLE
SURVIVORS OF SUICIDE
62 CLEVELAND AVE.
RUTLAND, VT 05701
(802) 775-5595

VIRGINIA

HELEN FITZGERALD
SUICIDE SURVIVOR SUPPORT
8119 HOLLAND RD.
ALEXANDRIA, VA 22306
(703) 273-3454

JO MOSS
SUICIDE SURVIVORS
SUPPORT
107 W. MAIN ST.
DANVILLE, VA 24541
(804) 724-4541

CHRIS GILCHRIST
SURVIVORS OF SUICIDE
4811 W. HIGH ST.
PORTSMOUTH, VA
(804) 483-3404

LEEANN LANE-MALBON
SURVIVORS OF SUICIDE
1701 WILL-O-WISP DR.
VIRGINIA BEACH, VA 23454
(804) 468-3655

CHRIS GILCHRIST
SURVIVORS OF SUICIDE
3210 CHURCHLAND BLVD.
CHESAPEAKE, VA 23321
(804) 483-3404

SUICIDE-CRISIS CENTER
P.O. BOX 1493
PORTSMOUTH, VA 23705
(804) 393-0502

PENNY GINGER
SURVIVING
900 E. BROAD ST., RM. 406
RICHMOND, VA 23219
(804) 780-5876

WASHINGTON

TRISH BLANCHARD
SURVIVORS OF SUICIDE
1515 DEXTER AVE. N., #300
SEATTLE, WA 98109
(206)461-3222

RICHARD NORDGREN
SURVIVORS OF SUICIDE
7525 W. DESCHUTES PL. S., #2A
KENNEWICK, WA 99336
(509)783-7416

CAROLYN BONDY
SURVIVORS OF SUICIDE
3330 N. VILLARD
TACOMA, WA 98407
(206)759-5168

CYNTHIA FREEMAN
SURVIVING SUICIDE
4710 PLOMONDON ST., #65
VANCOUVER, WA 98661
(206)694-7468

WEST VIRGINIA

EMMA WILKINS
SUICIDE SURVIVORS
SUPPORT
P.O. BOX 4043
WHEELING, WV 26003
(304)277-3916

WISCONSIN

KAREN BORK
SURVIVORS OF SUICIDE
537 N. SUPERIOR ST.
APPLETON, WI 54911
(414)739-1231

DON & JONNA BOSTEDT
SURVIVORS OF SUICIDE
630 GREENE AVE.
GREEN BAY, WI 54301
(414)437-7527

MARCIA WILLIAMS
SURVIVORS HELPING SURVI-
VORS
2900 W. OKLAHOMA
MILWAUKEE, WI 53215
(414)649-6000

PAM HERTEL
SUICIDE LOSS SUPPORT
2629 N. 7TH ST.
SHEBOYGAN, WI 53083
(414)458-3951

JEANNE ADAMS
SURVIVORS OF SUICIDE
625 W. WASHINGTON AVE.
MADISON, WI 53703
(608)251-2345

DIANE MIDLAND
KARIS
1910 SOUTH AVE.
LA CROSSE, WI 54601
(608)785-0530

CLARITA SELZ
SUICIDE SURVIVORS SUP-
PORT GROUP
900 W. CLAIREMONT AVE.
EAU CLAIRE, WI 54701
(715)839-4349

WILLIAM HUBMANN
SURVIVORS
611 ST. JOSEPH AVE.
MARSHFIELD, WI 54449
(715)387-7753

BIBLIOGRAPHY

Brodie, Gilbert. *Death Studies* 12 (1988): 147-71.

Dublin, Louis. *Suicide: A Sociological and Statistical Study.* New York: Ronald Press Co., 1963.

Durkheim, Emile. *Suicide.* Glencoe, Illinois: Free Press, 1951.

Farmer, R.D.T.. *British Journal of Psychiatry* 153 (1988): 16-20.

Garfinkel, B. D.. *American Journal of Psychiatry* 139 (1982): 1257-1261.

Gauqelin, Michael. *How Atmospheric Conditions Affect Your Health.* New York: Stein and Day, 1971.

Hewett, J.H.. *After Suicide.* Philadelphia: Westminster Press, 1980.

Klerman, Gerald. *British Jounal of Psychiatry* 152 (1988): 4-14.

Menninger Perspective 4 (1988): 5.

Ryn, Zdzislaw. *Suicide & Life Threatening Behavior* 16 (1986): 419-433.

Sekaer, Christina. *American Journal of Psychotherapy* 41 (1987): 201-19.

Shneidman, Edwin. *Voices of Death.* New York: Harper & Row, 1980.

Shneidman, Edwin. *Suicide & Life Threatening Behavior* 15 (1985): 51-55.

Simpson, Eileen. *Orphans Real and Imaginary.* New York: Weidenfeld & Nicolson, 1987.

Sumner, William Graham. *Folkways.* Boston: Ginn & Co, 1906.

Van der Wal, Jan. Paper given at Second European Symposium on Suicidal Behavior, Edinburgh, May 29 - June 1, 1988.

Westermarck, Edward. *Sociological Review* 1 (1908): 12-33.

Wrobleski, Adina. *OMEGA: Journal of Death and Dying* 15 (1984): 173-84.

About the author

Rita Robinson is an award-winning journalist specializing in medicine and psychology. A member of the American Medical Writers Association, she conducts writer's workshops for colleges and professional groups. Her home is in the mountain community of Lytle Creek, California.

A New Age Handbook On Death and Dying

Rev. Carol W. Parrish-Harra

The author shares insights from her ministries with terminally ill patients and their families; from her near-death experience, and from her grief following the sudden loss of her daughter and granddaughter. Both lay persons and profes-sionals can trust this authoritative work.

Rev. Carol Parrish-Harra is the highly respected founder of the Light of Christ Community Church and Seminary. Listed in Who's Who of American Women and Who's Who in the World, her ministry takes her all over the globe.

160 pp. • ISBN 0-9616605-4-6 • tradepaper • $9.95 Item #103

Name _____

Address _____

City _____ State _____ Zip _____

☐ Please send me a **free** catalog of books, cassettes and videos.

QTY	TITLE/DESCRIPTION	UNIT PRICE	TOTAL
	Survivors of Suicide	$9.95	
	Stepping Stones to Grief Recovery	8.95	
	Gifts for the Living...	9.95	
	The New Age Handbook on Death and Dying	9.95	
	AIDS: A Self-Care Manual	14.95	
	When Someone You Love Has AIDS	8.95	

SUBTOTAL	
SALES TAX 6.5% (CA residents)	
SHIPPING/HANDLING	
TOTAL	

Shipping/Handling Charges

$ 0.01 - $15.00...add $2.00
  15.01 - 26.00...add 4.00
  26.01 - 35.00...add 5.00
  35.01 - 46.00...add 6.00
  46.01 - 60.00...add 8.00
  60.01 - 100.00...add 10.00
 100.01 - 200.00...add 15.00
 200.01 - 300.00...add 20.00

QUANTITY DISCOUNTS
AVAILABLE
(213) 450-6485

Please send check or money order to:

IBS PRESS
744 Pier Avenue, Santa Monica, CA 90405
(213) 450-6485

IBS PRESS
744 Pier Avenue
Santa Monica, CA 90405